Lead the change you want to see in your school, your country and your world.

Teachers and school leaders are the best creators of innovation and change in education, yet often their ideas do not get the support they need to positively impact students. It's time for that to change. Now it's *your* turn.

Edupreneur is your inspirational guide to bringing change to education. Authors Aaron Tait and Dave Faulkner have helped educators all over the world build better schools from the classroom up—and now you can use their proven tools to bring your own ideas to life.

You already know the *what* and the *why*. This practical guide teaches you the *how*. Learn to:

- identify your driving passion as an educator with crystal clarity
- focus on the problems that most need solving in your school
- dig down to understand the root causes of issues
- innovate powerful solutions to the problems you have identified
- turn your best ideas into real actions that change the lives of your students
- share your ideas across the school and the wider education sector.

Edupreneur will help you bring change to your school.

Become an Edupreneur.

Edupreneur

Edupreneur

UNLEASHING **TEACHER-LED INNOVATION** IN SCHOOLS

Aaron Tait and Dave Faulkner

Typeset in 12.5/15.5 pt Adobe Garamond Pro

National Library of Australia Cataloguing-in-Publication data:

Creator:	Tait, Aaron, author.
Title:	Edupreneur: unleashing teacher-led innovation in schools / Aaron Tait, Dave Faulkner.
Subjects:	Educational innovations. Educational change.
Other Creators/ Contributors:	Faulkner, David, author.
Dewey Number:	371.956

Disclaimer

To the edupreneurs, teachers and school leaders who work every day to provide a great education for their students.

Contents

First things first

The edupreneurs we search for

'Right now, this is the most challenging school in the country, and we want you to be its new principal.'

Dave was twenty-seven when he received this phone call.

Two years later, a planeload of school and system leaders, philanthropists and education experts landed on the dusty outback runway near his school. With notepads in hand, they asked him how the school had been turned around so quickly.

They wanted to know what the solution had been at this school, so they could also apply it elsewhere. But Dave's answer was not what they expected.

'If you want to know the answers, I can give you some of them, but the majority of them will come from my team.'

Dave had spent two years creating an environment among his staff, students and community where they all felt like they could identify problems in the school, create solutions to these problems and make things better.

Aaron received a similar call to Dave's when he was twenty-five.

'This school is broken. We want you to come and lead it.'

A year later, he left the East African school and slum he had called home, content that the school had seen dramatic improvements in attendance, student wellbeing and achievement, and staff retention. He also knew that the best solutions had not come from him; rather, his role had been to create an environment where everyone in the school was solving problems and getting better, every day.

In 2010, we were both invited to speak at a conference. Aaron was a social entrepreneur, working to improve the lives of people living in extreme poverty in Africa with his organisation Spark* International.

Dave was the director of what is likely the world's largest education region, near the famous Uluru in Australia.

Over a drink later that day, we traded stories of schools that we had led, and realised that our leadership approaches were almost identical. Early in our careers we had both realised that our job as leaders was to unleash the passion and innovation of our staff, rather than try to solve all of the problems ourselves. At the time, Aaron was trying to unleash grassroots innovation at scale by finding and backing entrepreneurs in very poor communities, and Dave was trying to build a movement of innovative and highly effective teachers and school leaders across his region. We were doing the same thing, in different parts of the world. We now wondered if we could work together to build something great. We called the idea 'edupreneurship' and made a plan for Aaron to travel to the outback a few months later to spend time with some of Dave's best teachers to help them lead improvements in their schools.

That night we had no idea that the word 'edupreneur' had been coined more than a decade before. The next morning, Aaron typed the word into Google and read that it had come into popularity in the early 2000s, and was used to describe tech entrepreneurs, often with MBAs, who had built education websites for kids. We had huge respect for these kinds of people and knew they were doing great things for education, but this was not what we had been talking about! The term had been hijacked!

We wanted to see if we could bring the energy and innovation of the startup world into schools and unleash teacher-led innovations; brilliant ideas created by teachers who worked in classrooms and worked every day to change things for kids.

So we got to work. We started with fifteen teachers. We gave them some tools and the confidence to identify problems in their schools, propose solutions, engage people behind those solutions, and change things.

And change things they did.

We were blown away. We saw attendance rates go from 40 to 90 per cent. We saw teacher retention, student wellbeing, outcomes and community engagement change rapidly. We started to spend time with schools that needed 'turning around' as well as with very strong schools that simply had a commitment to get better every day, and we found that the same conditions were necessary for success. And those conditions were simple. School leaders and the education system needed to create an environment where teachers had the confidence and the capacity to continually identify challenges in their schools, try to search for relevant, local solutions and, if they worked, be encouraged to share their successes.

Since starting with this original group of fifteen teachers, we have worked with thousands of teachers and school leaders to bring the speed, creativity and risk-taking of entrepreneurship into staffrooms and classes around world. And we are doing this because we truly believe that entrepreneurial leaders can provide some of the best solutions for positive change in the world. The more people there are standing up and deciding that they are not happy with the status quo, and building solutions — either as business entrepreneurs, social entrepreneurs or intrapreneurs within organisations — the better the world we can create together.

The economist Joseph Schumpeter defined entrepreneurs as the 'creative destructors necessary for major advances'. We do what we do because we believe that education needs more people like this — people who aren't afraid of identifying problems and building game-changing solutions to address them.

So in this book, we are reclaiming the word 'edupreneur' to define any teacher or school leader who looks at their classroom, their school or their community and says, 'This could be better, and I am going to do something about it'.

Chances are, if you have opened this book, you are someone who thinks like this.

Edupreneur is a book designed to inspire and equip you to make the changes that you want to see in your school, your country, your world.

A generation of kids is waiting for your next move.

Make it count.

~~What?~~

~~Why?~~

HOW?

Plenty of thought leaders in education are jetted around the world in business class from conference to conference. Their role is to disrupt our thinking as educators and to help us dream of new possibilities. They inspire us. They make us question things.

Your job as a teacher or school leader is much harder—because you need to turn ideas into practical solutions.

No doubt you come back from conferences or professional development opportunities inspired by the thought leaders on the stage. Perhaps you even buy their books or tweet the links to their TED talks.

But how long does the post-conference high last?

Maybe you return to school and are bombarded by curriculum changes, reports, parent–teacher meetings and behaviour issues? You know that things should be better, but you are so busy putting out spot fires that you never get around to leading the change you want to see. You become reactionary rather than being revolutionary.

Then a few months later, you see another inspiring keynote speech online or at a conference and you hear again that things need to change. You gasp in unison with the rest of the audience at the photos of a classroom from last century next to one from today, shocked that nothing has changed. You hear the words 'industrial education system'. You eyeball yet more graphs with lines sloping downwards, rather than going up. You get told over and over that education needs to change.

The thing is, we all know making changes in education is complex and tough. We all know *what* needs to change and *why* it needs to be changed.

What is missing is the *how*.

This book helps with that. We have spent years working in schools and know that the education sector is incredibly complex. But rather than adding complexity, we are taking a step in the other direction.

As Ernest Schumacher said in his awesome book *Small is Beautiful: A Study of Economics As If People Mattered*, 'Any intelligent fool can make things bigger, more complex and more violent. It takes a touch of genius—and a lot of courage to move in the opposite direction.'

We truly believe that making change in schools can be broken down into a few simple and clear steps that you can get stuck into with your staff, students and parents today.

In *Edupreneur*, we present the tools and ideas that you and your team can draw on to identify challenges, come up with great solutions, mobilise people behind them and change things. The Changemaker Journey has been created by us as we have tried to lead changes in schools and been galvanised by working alongside thousands of teachers and school leaders over the last few years.

So given our belief that the *how* can often be very simple, we have written *Edupreneur* in as simple and fun a style as possible.

If you are looking for an academic book, where every second sentence is referenced and a third of the book is made up of references and further reading, you will not find it in *Edupreneur*. It is not a thesis that has been turned into a hardback; it is a play-by-play guide that has been developed over years in schools and classrooms. This is deliberate—because we want this book to be read, by teachers.

See, the funny thing is that the thesis that Aaron wrote at Cambridge (which he is proud to say he received a high distinction for, but is less proud to say he now struggles to understand) was only read by himself and his examiner (although his wife very kindly read the introduction). We hope that many more people will read this book, however, and have decided to write it as if we are having a great chat with you in the staffroom at lunch. This means we sometimes start sentences with 'and' and 'but'—and we would like to extend our deepest apologies to English teachers around the world (who are probably wriggling uncomfortably in their seats!).

So treat this book more like your favourite old t-shirt, rather than the shoes you bought for your wedding and never wore again. Write all over it. Take it around with you. The older and more worn it gets, the more value it has had for you. If you think it is useful, give your copy to a teacher on your staff, and see what ideas they come up with.

Edupreneur is more Jamie Oliver, less Heston Blumenthal. The ideas in here are things that you can get started on today, with all the bits and bobs you already have in your cupboard, instead of something you need a decade of training in Michelin-starred kitchens to grasp.

It's also more of a road map than a guidebook. The next time you are in school and it feels like the thing you were trying to change is all going wrong, open this book up, get an injection of inspiration and figure out where you are on your journey. We are not going to tell you the must-see museum, or the one route you need to take; rather, we are giving you the tools you need to build your own journey, and create your own solutions.

We work with thousands of teachers and school leaders every year with these ideas, and when they really go for it as edupreneurs they truly do amazing things.

Like the young teacher who kept her proud old public school open by turning it into a specialist beach volleyball centre; the kids are now thriving academically, even though they have beach sand between their toes. Or the teacher who figured out how to provide a world-class education in a rough township at a fraction of the cost of nearby schools. Or the teacher who committed to making 'class time more fun than playtime' and massively changed the learning outcomes of her kids in the process. Or the maths teacher who loved maths but hated the bad rap it always got, so committed to building a movement of educators who would share ways to help kids fall in love with maths. Or the two teachers who worked to make sure new teachers were happy and thriving in their first year in the profession. Or the teacher who said to head office, 'Give me the worst behaved kids in the region, and I will build a school for them.'

Throughout this book you will meet educators like this. If you are already one of them, you have found a new tribe to join. If you are just starting out, welcome. We can't wait to see what you build.

YES	NO
Fun	Tiring
Engaging	Boring
Easy	Hard
Practical	Abstract

Can your swimming instructors swim?

Imagine you didn't know how to swim but wanted to learn. You hear about an organisation that is offering swimming lessons and you sign up.

You go along to the class and find out that the teacher has never swum before. They take you through a slide show that outlines the concepts behind swimming and some pointers on what to do if you get in trouble, and show you videos of amazing swimmers winning gold medals at the Olympics. You don't get in the pool during the class and, at the end, they wish you luck in your swimming career.

You don't feel too comfortable about swimming yet, so you look for more classes. You go to a few of them, and they all have nice marketing and cool websites, but they teach you the same thing as the first one you went to, and you still don't get in the pool.

Then imagine one day, you go to a swimming class, your instructor can swim and, after a quick briefing, they have you jump in the pool. At first you struggle, floundering your way around the pool, swallowing water and trying to figure out how to stay afloat (and not remembering anything from the educational slide shows). Your instructor is there and can help you if you are really sinking, but they know that you will learn quicker the less they hold onto you. They can yell out some tips to you, but it is up to you to listen to them, and choose which ones you want to take on board.

In this book, we are your swimming instructors. We know how to swim—we have used these techniques to stay afloat and win races before.

So who are we?

After finishing high school Dave, with a burning desire to make a difference in the tough communities he had grown up in, decided to become a teacher. While still in university he headed out to a severely disadvantaged community as an intern teacher and put his hand up to teach the most difficult class. This trend continued, and with each transfer and promotion Dave volunteered for the most challenging jobs. The young people in the toughest settings were his *why*; indeed, the harder the kids were to reach, the more determined he was to reach them. He was appointed a principal at age twenty-four, and that same year he became a father. Over the next twelve years Dave, with his young family alongside him every step of the way, worked across a number of the most challenging communities in Australia. He worked tirelessly day after day—driving the school bus at seven in the morning to pick up students, for example, and working late into the night to create better opportunities for those students. As Dave's own children reached school age, people would often comment, 'Are you not worried about your kids' education in these difficult schools that you run?', to which he would always respond, 'If the school I lead isn't good enough for my kids, it isn't good enough for any kid'.

Aaron brings a different skill set to the partnership. He also grew up wanting to make a difference in the world, but dreamed of doing it as a peacekeeper. He joined the military in 2001 as a seventeen year old with the goal of one day wearing a blue UN beret, but was deployed to Iraq the day after 9/11 and served in active and often very hostile operations. He stayed in the military for seven years as an officer, spending his spare time when he was home from operations completing two master's degrees, or in favelas, townships and slums around the world trying to help people living in poverty. After leaving the military he ran a secondary school for orphans and street kids in Tanzania, built an orphanage for HIV/AIDS orphans in Kenya and completed a third research master's at Cambridge University. With his wife, Kaitlin, he co-founded Spark* International—an organisation that has backed hundreds of social entrepreneurs in Africa and Asia. With these social entrepreneurs he has helped change the lives of hundreds of thousands of people living in poverty through the creation of a job, the building of a home or supporting someone to significantly improve health or education.

We started Education Changemakers (EC) in 2012 with a goal of helping build a generation of teachers and school leaders with the confidence and skills to change the game for millions of children. Throughout *Edupreneur* we share a few of our practical stories of leading change in education, giving you an insight into both our failures and successes.

The EC tribe is made up of thousands of passionate teachers from around the world who have helped to improve and refine the ideas in this book. These teachers include heroes like Summer Howarth and Louka Parry from Australia, Jeff Li in Harlem, Chris Bradford in Johannesburg, Jabiz Raisdana in Singapore and Laura McBain from High Tech High in San Diego. And now that you are reading this book, we can welcome you to the EC tribe as well! Perhaps in our next book, we will be telling your story?

Many of these teachers like to hang out on Twitter, so feel free to join the conversation using #educhange.

Now, we are almost ready to get you to jump in the pool.

It's a journey

Trying to solve problems and make things better can often feel overwhelming. But friends, this little Changemaker Journey (overleaf) that we have built makes things much easier! We think it is an awesome play-by-play guide to help you unleash great ideas in your school. At any point, you can move back or forward in the journey, and checking in with it is a nice way to see where you are at. You will see us link back to this journey throughout the book, and it will all make a lot more sense to you very soon!

1. What am I passionate about?

2. We believe...

3. But right now the reality is...

4. What are the root causes?

5. Other players?

6. Focus on one root cause.

7. Ideate fifty solutions.

8. Prototype the best two.

9. Test the best.

10. Pivot or persevere.

11. Turn the idea into something real.

12. Prove it gets results.

13. Make it scalable and sustainable.

14. Take it to scale and change many lives.

15. Return to step 1 or retire.

How to use this book

Well, ultimately, that is up to you to decide.

You can read this book all the way through, get a blast of inspiration and ideas, and then refer back to it when you need to.

Or you can do what you often try to get your kids to do and learn by doing, a little bit at a time, trusting the process and only moving on as you complete each step.

It's totally your call.

You may choose to write all over this book (in fact, if you send us a picture of your copy covered in annotations and sticky notes we will tweet it!).

Perhaps you will use it to create new solutions to old problems. To focus on what matters. To turn your passionate ideas into awesome realities. To help you collaborate with the brilliant minds in your staffroom. To create the changes you know your students need.

You might grab bits. You might love it all.

You might absolutely hate it, scream, 'This is not an academic text!' and stop reading at this page. If your copy is an ebook, you can easily deal with your frustrations—just delete the file and free up some space on that tablet of yours. If it's an old-fashioned paperback, make sure you put it to good use as a doorstop, shred it up to make kitty litter or add it to the pile keeping your computer screen at the right height.

Still with us? Great! We do have one little favour to ask before you delve in.

We know that you are busy. So busy that often you don't have time to read a book like this and invest in yourself.

But we have made this as easy a read as possible.

So take a bit of time out.

Maybe a few good hours on a weeknight or a Sunday afternoon. Turn off the laptop, stop checking your emails, pour yourself a glass of something (or make a cup of tea) and soak up some new ideas. Every time you get a new idea for your school, write it down. You might find yourself grabbing this whole process and trying all of it with your team, or you might just grab a few concepts.

If you come up with a cool idea that improves the learning outcomes of the kids in your class, that is awesome, and the book has achieved its aim. If you spread that idea to other classes and other schools, that is super awesome!

You might be coming into this book with an idea that you are already working on, or with nothing at all. The approach is the same for both and we encourage you to trust the process.

So what do you need to get started?

It's pretty simple, really. All you need is:

- an open mind
- trust in the process
- some sticky notes (or just rip up some small squares of paper)
- a pen.

Turn it into
something great.

↑

Create something
good.

↑

Start with nothing.

Dream

'Teachers matter ... grant schools flexibility: to teach with creativity and passion ...'

US President Barack Obama

Me? An edupreneur?

We believe passionately that the best solutions for education come from teachers. Seems obvious really, doesn't it? But the reality is education systems across the globe are still a long way from being defined by teacher-led innovations.

Let's jump into a radical metaphor quickly. If you are trying to get a better result from your football team, you can try out lots of things. You can renovate the stadium—making the grass greener and the team areas more comfortable. You can invest in some nice new uniforms, or better physiotherapists. You can give the players more sports drinks so that they are better hydrated during the game. But, on game day, the one thing that really matters is how they play. Do they turn up alert and fired up? Do they play with creativity and passion? Do they push themselves the extra 5 per cent they need to win? If the answers are yes, they might just do enough to get the points they need to win. If they don't perform, all of that other stuff is superfluous.

Teachers are like those players. They can only hit the home runs they need to win tomorrow if they turn up and play their hearts out. We can try to give them new classrooms, or technology, or short injections of professional development, but really what they need is the license to go out there on game day, give it their all, and play with passion and creativity.

That's why we do what we do, and why we wrote this book.

So is this book relevant for school or system leaders, even though they are more like the coaches and the administration on the team?

Without a doubt.

As a principal, Dave learned that his job was to create an environment and culture in his school that unleashed, supported and sometimes just got out of the way of his edupreneurs as they stood up and made things better. To paraphrase Lao Tzu, a leader is best when people barely know she exists—when her work is done, her aim fulfilled, they will say: we did it ourselves. Just as a great classroom must have a great teacher, a truly great school must have great leadership that empowers all staff to learn, grow and teach effectively.

And what about at the system level? Are we calling for anarchy there, promoting the idea that teachers have got this and they should be left alone?

Absolutely not.

Some things will always need to have oversight from a central office. Academics, administrators, superintendents and politicians can help to create the environment needed for teachers to allow great things to come into play, and also identify pockets of brilliance and help them scale. What we are calling for is an even greater license for teachers and leaders to take risks and search for the solutions that will change the game for kids.

We believe that to consistently make schools better we need the system, school leaders and teachers all working together. Listening to each other. Coming up with great ideas. Today, tomorrow and the day after, and every day after that.

You can come up with plenty of excuses as to why you might not think you can stand up and be an edupreneur. One that we hear all the time is, 'But I'm a teacher. I can't do all this entrepreneurship stuff.'

We are going to try to convince you otherwise.

JK Rowling was an English teacher who thought it was unacceptable that kids weren't reading enough. So she wrote Harry Potter, a book series that helped a fair few kids (and adults probably) finish a novel for the first time in their lives.

Steve Wozniak wanted to unleash the creativity of a generation, and thought that technology could be a great way to do it. His work co-founding Apple did a pretty good job in this department and, when he left, he *began* teaching in primary schools. Amazing.

Hugh Jackman used to be a gym teacher who was passionate about his students eating well and living healthy lives. Now as Wolverine in *X-Men* he has inspired a generation of kids to grow big muscles and hold forks in between their fingers (and maybe inspired a few mothers and fathers to be healthier as well!).

Anita Roddick was a teacher who was passionate about the environment and started making soap out of ethical ingredients in her spare time. At the time of writing, The Body Shop has 2500 stores around the world and has given almost $100 million to charity.

A few more interesting characters who started as teachers include Sylvester Stallone, Sheryl Crow, Mr T, Sting and Gene Simmons from KISS. (We pity the fools who were in Mr T's gym classes!)

Of course, we are not saying that you need to go out and launch a business or become a famous musician or actor, but what we are saying is back yourselves, teachers! Teachers are awesome human beings!

Another one we hear often is, 'I would love to do all this, but the system needs to be changed.' What is funny is that people always think the grass is greener somewhere else. In Australia they say, 'Yeah, it is easy for them in the US, but we can't do all that stuff here because the system doesn't let us.' In the United States we hear, 'Yeah, it is easy for them in Australia, but we can't do all that stuff here because the system doesn't let us.'

The 'system' is a funny thing, isn't it? It is all around us, yet no-one really knows who actually drives it. Sounds a bit like the matrix! We think it is better to light a candle than curse the darkness. Get started, solve problems and change things. The 'system' (by which we mean the head office in your zone or district and the politicians who are telling them what to do) needs wins. People's jobs are on the line and if you are getting results, you are going to make them happy.

Dave worked in the 'system' for a number of years and he'll tell you passionately that many of the barriers we so often talk about in schools don't really exist. The secret is, the system is nothing without the teachers within it.

When we ask the best edupreneurs we know how the 'system' let them make the changes they did, they all have the same response: 'Oh, I just did it.' They prefer to ask for forgiveness rather than permission. And as principal (and TEDxMelbourne speaker) Peter Hutton says, 'In order to break the rules, you need to know them better than anyone else.' Some of the best edupreneurs even stake their jobs and careers on decisions they make, knowing that great results provide a great way to change the minds of even the toughest critics.

Now take a second. When is the last time you took a breath in your class and thought to yourself, *Wow, that really worked*?

We all know that brilliant researchers and experts are out there collecting evidence about what good practice looks like on our behalf as teachers. They just never seem to come into our classes, do they? Rarely as teachers are we invited to the conference stage to share frankly about the best class we have ever taught, or the learning concept that knocked our socks off.

Sometimes it can feel pretty lonely tucked away in a Year 5 classroom in the suburbs. Or during a Thursday final period class. It can feel like maybe no-one will ever see the magic of your kids learning, or you smashing a class that you spent your Sunday evening preparing. Rarely, if ever, will an expert be at the back of your room, nodding and giving you a thumbs up.

Or perhaps we start to feel like we are doing okay, and then a new piece of research presented at a conference makes us think otherwise. Or some standardised test scores from that one hour, on that one day, suggest your class is way behind where they should be. It sucks that these confidence-sapping moments can often dispel the great moments. Like when the frustrated kid who always prefers to sit closest to the window made the connection between natural resource degradation and impoverished communities. We all know that a multiple choice test will never give her a chance to share her learning about that.

Have you ever stopped backing yourself?

Don't. You've got this. You can continue to do amazing things in your school. And never forget: what's ordinary to you may be extraordinary to others.

So read on; let's hang out and share stories of teaching and learning. Let's do something great together. Welcome to the #educhange movement.

Did your school take a step forwards or a step backwards today?

Our school doesn't need to innovate

If you have been thinking, *Our school is great and doesn't need to be 'turned around', we don't really need all this edupreneur stuff*, think again.

Ray Kroc, the man who established McDonald's as the global company it is today, once asked, 'Are you green and growing or ripe and rotting?' So this kind of thinking is what is often now called 'ripe and rotting' thinking. You may be sweet now, but in a couple of days the brown spots will start forming.

Think about some of the following lessons from history of people who thought they were sweet.

Cambridge Professor Douglas Hartree is famous for saying in 1951 that all the calculations that would ever be needed in England could be done on the three digital computers which were then being built. 'No-one else would ever need machines of their own, or be able to afford to buy them.'

Oh, Professor, how wrong you were.

Take yourself back a few years, to 2004. Imagine it is a cold Saturday night and rather than heading out to a bar or restaurant with friends you wanted nothing more than a night in watching a movie. Perhaps you walked to the nearest Blockbuster video store, looking for *Shrek 2* (the most popular film that year). You noticed that they were all rented, and so browsed the aisles for something else that took your fancy. (*Meet the Fockers* was another hit that year, maybe you grabbed that one?) Pretty much all of us were members of video stores back then. But in 2010, Blockbuster went bust. How quickly things changed.

In 2012 Kodak, for decades one of the world's most iconic companies, also went bankrupt.

When was the last time you bought a cassette tape for your car? Or a CD for that matter? Or even downloaded a song on iTunes?

The world is changing and even the schools that have traditionally been the best can't rest on their laurels. Around the world we are seeing education models disrupted either by ambitious (and often controversial) public or charter schools taking enrolments away from private schools, or through scalable models like Bridge International Academies in Africa or free online platforms like Kahn Academy.

So if the thought came to you that your school doesn't need to innovate, we think this is dangerous thinking. The tools in this book, and the idea of dreaming big for a new future, apply to you just as much as they do to a school that is doing it tough.

As Steve Jobs famously reminded us, 'Stay hungry, stay foolish'.

'He who has a why to live by can bear almost any how.'

Friedrich Nietzsche

Your *why*

In 2007 Aaron left the military, and he and his wife, Kaitlin, sold most of what they owned, handed back the keys to their apartment in Sydney and took a one-way flight to East Africa. After three months in Kenya, during some of the worst violence the country has seen in decades, they moved to Tanzania to lead a secondary school for street kids.

They settled into the slum that was to be their new home and got to work. Every morning they would wake up with smiles on their faces, make a cup of strong black coffee, blast their cheap little radio with local tunes and get fired up for a day trying to bring change to a bunch of kids who really needed it.

They set themselves some big goals—the biggest being the target of at least ten of the senior kids getting through the national exams and into university. In a school where only one student had achieved this in the three previous years, the odds were against them. An already tough job was made even tougher in the first six months, with each of them suffering five bouts of malaria; and being subject to investigations from the police (who suspected they were CIA), curses from local witchdoctors (underperforming staff members would often spend their final pay cheque putting a curse on Aaron) and even a handful of pretty serious death threats (more on that later).

Aaron's parents came to visit the school when the couple had been there for almost a year and, when they saw how Aaron and Kaitlin were living, sat them down and told them how worried they were that they were going to die in the slum. His parents were passionate, compassionate and well-travelled people, but they found it hard to understand why Aaron and Kaitlin were pushing so hard.

But Aaron and Kaitlin knew their *why*.

They loved the kids in the school. They were their *why*. When they had first moved to the slum, they were shocked by the reality that two in five people had HIV/AIDS and that four in five kids didn't finish high school. They felt that the school could be a beacon of hope in the community, and they were desperate to do what they could to try to make sure that hope was realised. So they fought for it with everything they had, and it almost killed them.

We love the line from Friedrich Nietzsche quoted earlier: 'He who has a why to live by can bear almost any how'. It means that if you know why you are doing what you're doing—why you're getting up each day and going back in to fight for something—you can get over all the barriers that come your way. And as an edupreneur, there will definitely be barriers!

We often say that 'your why should make you cry'. You should care so much about what you are fighting for that really thinking about it, the people you are serving and the future you hope for, brings tears to your eyes. Later in the book we will check in with Aaron and see if his *why* was strong enough to figure out the *how* of leading change in the school.

Do you know your *why*?

Check-in

Okay. Let's check in and see how you are doing. Chances are, you are one of two types of people:

- *Person 1:* As soon as we asked you what your *why* was, you knew straightaway. Awesome. Keep powering through the next few pages to get even more clarity and focus about what it is that makes you fight so hard for change in your school.
- *Person 2:* You really struggled on that last page. You don't really know what your *why* is. If this is you, don't stress. Trust the process, because we are pretty confident that in just a few pages you are going to start to feel a lot more like Person 1.

So let's get back to it.

1. What am I passionate about?

Dream big

Nelson Mandela had a big dream for South Africa.

He was so passionate about his *why* that he spent twenty-seven years in jail trying to figure out a *how*.

He was a 'once in a generation' kind of leader.

The big question that Chris Bradford, a teacher from Michigan, kept asking was, 'What if leaders like him came around more often?'

He imagined a school that selected the smartest, most passionate and most innovative high school students from across Africa, regardless of their family's wealth, and brought them together for their first year of high school. He wondered whether, if these young leaders received the right education, they could be the ones who took their countries forward into a new reality.

He searched for a school like this across Africa but couldn't find one. He talked about his dream to anyone who would listen, and over and over he was told that he needed to talk to a guy called Fred Swaniker.

They met, realised they both shared the same vision for Africa, and a few years later the African Leadership Academy (ALA) was built in Johannesburg.

If you ever get the chance to walk around the campus of ALA you will marvel (like we did) at the incredibly intelligent kids who believe (and rightly so) that they can be nation leaders, and who have the potential and support to make it happen. (Check out africanleadershipacademy.org if you want to know more.)

It is a huge vision, but one that Chris, Fred and their team are working incredibly hard to make a reality. How big are you dreaming?

As Marianne Williamson said, 'Your playing small does not serve the world.'

We work with many teachers and school leaders every year. As we travel around the schools of the world, we hear a huge number of things that teachers find unacceptable.

Some of the statements that we hear are so bold, clear and inspired that they give us goosebumps.

But to be honest, some of them are a bit *blah*. We get the feeling that maybe that teacher can push for something bigger. Something that is really going to change a kid's life.

So we always challenge everyone to DO COOL STUFF.

When you think about your *why*, do you get excited? So excited that you can't wait to get stuck into the *how*? If your answer is YES, awesome. If it is NO, take some time to think about whether you are focused on the right thing.

Don't be afraid to take some time to think big, think new and think again.

Spending your time on something that doesn't inspire you is a waste of your passion and genius. Life is not a dress rehearsal and, before you know it, you will be old, whistling when you speak and spending your days playing bingo.

We are searching for dreamers. Not people who just say it like it is, but people who say it like it could be, and who do what it takes to get there.

People often say to us, 'Well, can you give me some examples of the types of teachers you are talking about?' Absolutely.

We're talking about people like Alyce Cleary, who helped to set up a fully functioning school within a prison; who believes that just because a young person is in trouble with the law, that doesn't mean they can't still make the most of every day as a learner. She sees the future, not the past. What that young person could be, not what they have been.

Or Jeff Li, who quit a high-flying corporate job to work as a maths teacher in Harlem.

Or Nonhlanhla Mesina, who opened a school in South Africa that operates at a third of the cost of the local public schools and whose kids are performing in the top tenth percentile of the country.

Or Kelly Tenkely, who takes smart (and sometimes crazy) risks at Anastasis College in always striving to give her kids a better education. (At Anastasis, for example, teachers report not just on what students have achieved, but also on how nice and creative they have been.)

Or Sergio Juárez Correa in Mexico, who spent his summer break re-thinking how he could teach his kids at a school where many of them failed. Twelve months later, one of his students achieved the best test score in the country.

Or, maybe, you?

Start with your class

Peter Thiel, the co-founder of PayPal (and a guy who snapped up 10 per cent of Facebook for half a million dollars), knows a thing or two about innovation. He refers to two different types of innovators: the 'zero to one' people and the 'one to two' people. The zero to one innovators are those who move from nothing to something game-changing. Think Thomas Edison inventing the lightbulb, or Elon Musk trying to get to Mars.

Then there are the one to two thinkers. The people who look at the way things already are and think, *I reckon we could do that better* (or cheaper, or quicker).

In this book, what are we talking about?

Well, you can use a lot of what is in here to come up with an idea that may fundamentally change the education sector, or how a part of the education system operates. If you come up with something like this, fantastic! Give yourself a pat on the back! Then please give us a call so we can help you scale it!

But really this book is best suited to educators around the world who look at education and say, *The status quo is not working, but rather than starting from scratch we need to keep making things better.* Going from zero to one takes years, and chances are you would have to leave your school to really make the idea happen. 'One to two' ideas, however, can come every day, and that's where we think you should start working. We want to be improving schools today. And tomorrow. And the day after that. That's what our kids need. A generation of teachers making small bets, getting small wins. The sum total of that is breathtaking and worthy of the Nobel Prize.

So we want you to think big, but act small to begin with.

'Each of us can work to change a small portion of events, and in the total of all those acts will be written the history of this generation.'

Robert F Kennedy

Don't start with a solution

Think of some of the most famous discoverers and inventors in history.

Archimedes sat in a bath and wondered why the water overflowed as he lowered himself down. His 'eureka' moment came from identifying a problem and trying to understand it. Same with Newton. As the legend goes, an apple fell on his head and then he tried to figure out why it was happening. When Edison invented the light bulb as we know it today, he didn't just think, *Light, now there's an idea!* He was trying to solve the challenge of darkness.

Lots of teachers come to us and say, 'Hey, I have this great idea', and our response is the same every time. 'What problem does it solve?'

Let's look at the invention of the gumboot.

An English guy called Hiram Hutchinson saw that French farmers wearing wooden clogs kept coming home with their feet wet and muddy.

He copied a boot design that the Duke of Wellington had made for war (that's why some people call the boots 'wellies' now), and decided he wanted to find a material that was both cheap and waterproof.

He found a guy called Charles Goodyear, who had just invented the process to make rubber, and, voila, the gumboot was invented.

Pretty simple, right?

Problem: farmers are getting their feet wet.

Solution: copy an old boot design, but use this cool new thing called rubber to make the boots waterproof and cheap.

Result: happy farmers and cashed up Hutchinson (although he looks a little grumpy in all the photos we've seen of him — search online and see for yourself).

Most entrepreneurs don't have 'light-bulb moments' where a staggeringly brilliant idea just pops into their head. Instead, they identify a problem that drives people nuts, understand it really well, and then try to find a really great solution.

So we are going to do the same, and jump into some problem identification for a little bit.

HEY! I HAVE THIS COOL IDEA.

(An edupreneur with a pretty low chance of succeeding.)

I THINK THIS COULD BE A GREAT SOLUTION TO A PROBLEM THAT MANY KIDS HAVE.

(An edupreneur with a much better chance of succeeding.)

Have a moan

So let's identify the problems that exist in your school. Let's find your equivalent of the grumpy French farmer with the wet and muddy feet.

Now, we can all easily slip into the guilty pleasure that comes with a good moan.

What we are going to give you here is the chance to indulge in a flurry of guilt-free complaining. We call them 'moaning minutes' and here is how they work:

1. Bring together a few people from your school community (definitely some teachers, but also think about including some parents, students and non-teaching staff). The more diverse your team here, the better (more on the importance of teams later in the book). If you are doing the session by yourself, that is fine as well.
2. Set a timer for five minutes. Have a pad of sticky notes and some pens. Play some tunes (we always love the Edwin Starr version of 'War' for this one).
3. Encourage your team to write down as many things they can think of that are not being done well in the school (or in education as a whole). Ask them to be as specific as they can here, and also to not hold back. Don't get personal, but feel free to write things like 'our parents are not interested in the school' or 'teachers are not working together well' or 'school is not fun'.

4 Once everyone is briefed, press go on the timer and get as many problems down as you can in five minutes. When the timer goes off, you are done! Try to keep the problem identification to this blast only (we don't need to have all these people in a room moaning for hours!).

If you want to get started before you bring a team together, feel free to throw in some comments in your Kindle or tablet, or on some sticky notes if you have a real book.

Moan here, please.

Focus your frustration

When Gandhi was doing his thing in India, guess what he started fighting first?

Salt.

He hated that the British would tax the Indian people to make salt. It made him furious. So he focused down to that issue, and began his historic salt march. A lot of issues made him angry, but the salt tax made him really, really angry. It gave him something to focus his frustration on.

So, you've just had a big moan.

You now have all these issues in front of you—all the things that currently suck in your school or in education more widely. Feels pretty huge, right? You might even have some things that seem insurmountable there.

But we all know that the best way to eat an elephant is one bite at a time.

So pick the one issue you want to solve the most.

Just one.

The one issue that really upsets you. That you always talk about in the staffroom (or at Friday drinks, or with your partner, your dog, or anyone who will listen, really).

Over the years, and after working with thousands of changemakers, we have found that the easiest way to figure out your *why* is to finish this sentence: 'It is unacceptable that...'

Gandhi thought the British tax on salt was unacceptable. What do you find unacceptable in your school or in education?

Don't complain about things you are not willing to change.

(By which we mean, make sure that your 'It is unacceptable that...' statement is something you are willing to be part of solving. Moaning minutes are over and we are almost at the point where we kick things into the positive!)

'It is UNACCEPTABLE that school is not fun for students.'

'It is UNACCEPTABLE that we are not preparing our kids for success in the real world.'

'It is UNACCEPTABLE that not all of our kids come to school every day.'

'It is UNACCEPTABLE that parents don't engage with the school.'

'It is UNACCEPTABLE that most kids in our school can't write a line of code.'

It is UNACCEPTABLE that...
(finish the sentence)

Justin Matthys, edupreneur

Justin loves maths.

For as long as he can remember, Justin has loved playing with numbers and trying to solve problems. He breezed through maths class in school, and then thrived doing advanced mathematics and astrophysics at university.

He is so good at maths that he was invited to work on the Higgs Boson experiment using the Large Hadron Collider (that big underground loop in Switzerland where they collide particles against each other at really fast speeds).

But he left this life to become a high school maths teacher in a public school in a challenging neighbourhood. And there he found that most kids didn't like maths. In fact, they were terrified of it, and this fear led to hatred. Justin says,

> I found it unacceptable that in my class of twenty-nine boys, only two of them really understood maths. The rest saw it as a dull set of recipes to be memorised and regurgitated as needed. I love maths; it has so much beauty and is so much fun to work with — to find connections, spot patterns, prove things and even just play. I was angry that most of my students had been robbed of this opportunity by being taught maths they weren't ready for, in the wrong way. I knew that true understanding in maths comes with the right practice at the right time — the problem was existing resources supported only rote learning, and the spread of abilities meant that each student was ready to learn something different at any given time (a practical impossibility in a class of twenty-nine).

Justin started working on Maths Pathways after the kids left each day, and because of this organisation there will be many more children in this world who will love maths as he does. And they will be the ones who create many of the things that our world needs (and maybe even bash particles against each other as well). Amazing job, Justin. (Check out www.mathspathway.com if you want to know more.)

What future are you fighting for?

When we think of the civil rights movement in the sixties in America, we often think of the famous leaders like Martin Luther King Jr and Rosa Parks who stood up (or sat down) and made a difference. Their names will forever be etched in the history books.

It wasn't all about them, though. The movement was really about the many people who believed in a better future for America and decided to do something about it. Because a movement is never about an individual. As Robert F Kennedy once said, 'Few will have the greatness to bend history itself, but each of us can work to change a small portion of events, and in the total of all of those acts will be written the history of this generation'. We like to call the people making these small changes the 'anonymous extraordinaires'.

The Greensboro Four were these kinds of people—willing to fight for a better future. On 1 February 1960, Joseph, Franklin, Ezell and David walked into a Woolworths store in Greensboro, North Carolina. They bought some things and then walked into the cafe for a coffee. When they were told that only whites could order in the cafe, they sat quietly for the rest of the day in a silent, non-violent protest. A quick search online will bring up a photo of them on that day. The next day they came back with twenty of their friends. The next day they brought sixty. The next day there were three hundred people. The protests then began to spread around the country.

Day after day, for months, thousands of people walked into segregated places across the US, and sat down for a new future. They believed in a free America and they were doing what they could to make it a reality. After a few months, they got the attention of the President, with Eisenhower saying, 'I am deeply sympathetic with the efforts of any group to enjoy the rights of equality that they are guaranteed by the Constitution'.

This was really tough work—particularly when people started pouring food and drinks on the protesters, sprinkling itching powder on them, or beating them up. But they kept on fronting up every day, because they believed in a free America, and they were willing to fight for it.

After turning up every day for six months, on 25 July three African American Woolworths employees were asked by their boss to change out of their uniforms and into their regular clothes and walk into the cafe and order food. They were served.

Many people think the Greensboro Four and their bold stand was what really catalysed the civil rights movement in the South. A few years later in 1964, the Civil Rights Act was passed. The next year the Voting Rights Act was passed (designed to prohibit racial discrimination in voting and enforce the voting rights guaranteed by the Fourteenth and Fifteenth Amendments to the United States Constitution). The country was still far from perfect, but it had changed.

We often wonder what it would feel like to know that you had been part of something so monumental in history. To know that you chose to do something that changed things for many people.

What would it be like to be an old man or an old woman, looking around at a community that was fundamentally different because of something you decided to do?

To know that your life was worth something. To know that you lived deliberately.

Well, another quick search online gives us a little taste of that feeling. You can see images of the Greensboro Four as old men, living in the future they helped create. In particular, you can find a photo of them sitting back at that Woolworth's lunch counter in 1990, drinking coffee.

Obviously, America is still far from perfect—to this day, race issues remain a real challenge in the country. But these four were part of something awesome, and (even though American coffee is not the greatest) we reckon that their coffees tasted pretty good on that day in 1990.

If this was their moment—when they could be proud of what they had achieved in their lives and take a moment to reflect back on the change they had made—what is yours going to look like?

Think ahead ten years from now. What are you seeing that is different? What changed? What will you be smiling about, knowing that you were part of making it a reality?

If these four young men were fighting for a free America, what are you fighting for? What future do you want to be part of creating?

The future you want to see in your school

Before you skip the page, write down a few notes here if you are reading a hardcopy book, on a sticky note if you are reading someone else's, or in a comment box if you are reading this electronically.

When Dave started as the principal at 'the most challenging school in Australia', he said, 'I am going to help create a school that I am happy to send my own kids to'. To put his money where his mouth was, he enrolled his kids in his school that day.

So get specific.

What are the sorts of things you are seeing when you walk around your school years from now?

Use the rest of this page to write about the future you want to fight for.

1. What am I passionate about?
2. We believe...

We believe

We love picking fights.

Not with people, but with problems.

We also love edupreneurs who identify big, compelling issues in education and then choose to do something about them.

So, by now you will have identified what it is that you find most unacceptable.

Now we get positive.

What does your school look like if you have solved that problem?

What is your Greensboro Four moment—where you are sitting there smiling, and looking back at what has changed?

As always, we keep things really simple. Just flip your 'It is unacceptable that…' statement and finish this sentence:

> 'We believe in a school/community/country/world where…'

We use *we* very deliberately. You are going to need lots of people on board who share this same dream to make it a reality.

'WE BELIEVE in a school where all of our kids love mathematics.'

'WE BELIEVE in a school where class time is more fun than playtime.'

'WE BELIEVE in a school where all of our students graduate prepared to excel as adults.'

'WE BELIEVE in a school where all of our parents are actively engaged in their child's learning.'

'WE BELIEVE in a school where all of our kids come to school every day.'

We believe...
(finish the sentence)

Maybe later

So maybe you are giving yourself some excuses why you can't start working on this just now. Did one of the following pass through your head?

- I am too busy.
- I need to get promoted first.
- This won't tie in with the curriculum.
- I haven't really led before.
- I am too young.
- I am too old.
- Some other excuse that is making you scared to do something awesome!

So here are some ideas to counteract these:

1. Think of the people who said no to dessert on the *Titanic* the night it sunk. Do cool things now, or it might be too late.
2. Go with your gut unless three people you trust tell you not to do it.
3. Do things that scare you.
4. Fear means go.
5. Remember the words of Aristotle: 'Where your talents and the needs of the world cross, there lies your vocation'.
6. Or Yogi Berra: 'When you come to a fork in the road, take it'.
7. And Gandhi: 'Live as if you were to die tomorrow; learn as if you were to live forever'.

Basically, your time is precious. Live deliberately.

Have you got it?

Friends, your 'We believe...' sentence is a very important little statement.

If you have yours figured out, you have what you need to move forward in the Changemaker Journey.

If you don't have it figured out yet, take a step back. See if you can nail down your 'It is unacceptable that...' statement, or even jump into a few more moaning minutes before you move to the next section.

Remember to trust the process here.

If you feel disrupted, like lots of big ideas are jumping around in your head, good. That means we are doing our job!

Now, let's switch from dreaming mode into digging mode.

Dig

The best way
to solve your
problems is
to understand
why they keep
happening.

Understand the problem

Let's imagine you think it is unacceptable that teachers aren't working together well at your school.

You come up with an inspiring vision of, 'We believe in a school where all teachers work together to achieve great results for all of our kids'.

At a staff meeting you stand up and proclaim this vision boldly and you are met with confusion and maybe even anger. Perhaps people don't agree that this is an issue. They think that they are working together just fine, thank you very much. Suddenly you feel like the new kid with no friends on your first day.

Maybe to make matters worse your principal shuts your dreaming down, telling you that right now you need to be focused on tests/reporting/curriculum changes/planning/*insert other annoying thing here*.

Before you even get started, you might find your idea is dead in the water.

You might get so frustrated that you give up, or start looking for another school to work in (or perhaps even another profession).

But with our support, you are not going to get to this point. We are going to teach you a few little tricks to help ensure that people get on board with your dream right from the beginning.

And the best way to start is to truly understand the problem.

As Einstein said, 'If I had an hour to solve a problem, I'd spend 55 minutes thinking about the problem and 5 minutes thinking about solutions'.

'Houston, we've had a problem.'

These words were first uttered by Jack Swigert on the Apollo 13 mission to the moon, and were then repeated by Jim Lovell. Houston didn't need much more convincing. But the easiest way to convince your team that a problem exists is to hit them with some numbers!

Let's say you were trying to back up your dream of 'A school where all teachers work together to achieve great results for all of our kids'. You could try some numbers like the following:

- 'The school that was named the best improving school in the region spends an average of three hours a week on teacher collaboration; we spend an average of two hours a month on it at our school.'
- 'In a quick survey of teachers at this school, 85 per cent of them said that they would be open to spending more time together planning and improving.'

You don't need to bring in a research team from a university or spend months doing a big study. Instead, try to find some compelling numbers online. Look at non-profit websites or education reports. Check out our website (ecstats.org). Maybe you could look at your school improvement plan or the latest report from head office. You could do some quick surveys in your school as well. You could also use anecdotal evidence (or, to put it more simply, tell some stories). For example, you might say, 'Hey team, I have been trying to get a team planning meeting going, and in a staff of 100, only three of you turned up to the last one—and I even put on free pizza! What are we doing wrong?'

So, the way that we frame this problem is to get you to finish the sentence, 'But right now the reality is…'. Dig up two or three punchy numbers to prove that a problem exists, and include them.

1. What am I passionate about?
2. We believe...
3. But right now the reality is...

But right now the reality is...
(insert compelling, juicy things here to prove that the problem exists)

Finding the killer

Dr Semmelweis was a Hungarian doctor working in Austria in the 1800s, with great sideburns and a passion for saving lives.

Semmelweis and his team of doctors found it unacceptable that so many mothers were dying in childbirth, from what they called 'childbed fever'. They believed in a hospital where every child would have the chance to grow up in good health. So he got to work trying to understand the reasons the number of deaths was so high.

After years of study, he found something pretty startling when he compared the findings from two different wards. In one ward, all births were conducted by male doctors and medical students. In the other ward, female midwives were in charge of the births. The rate of death in the ward run by the male doctors was five times higher than that of the female midwives' ward. This came as a shock, because the male staff were the highly educated, qualified doctors, and the female employees were the less qualified nurses. Semmelweis became obsessed with trying to figure out why there was such a difference between the two wards, and he came up with a few theories:

1. In the midwives' clinic, women gave birth on their sides — maybe this was better? They tried to get the male doctors to use this technique, but there was no improvement.
2. When someone died in the male ward, a priest would come and ring a bell. Perhaps the bell literally scared others to death? After this theory emerged, Semmelweis asked the priest to stop running his deadly bell. The deaths continued.

After a sustained run of failed innovations, Semmelweis decided to go away from the hospital for a while.

When he came back from his holidays, he wasn't met with good news. One of his closest friends had died while he was away, after pricking his finger with a scalpel he had been using during surgery on a woman. He was said to have died with the same symptoms that were associated with 'childbed fever'.

This was a little clue, because it meant that people other than women who had just given birth could contract 'childbed fever'. Semmelweis thought that maybe little things had travelled between the mother and the doctor when he was pricked. He thought that if doctors washed their hands, they could rid themselves of these dangerous little things.

Semmelweis was onto something big.

Well, something tiny actually.

Semmelweis was on the brink of understanding what germs (or bacteria) were, and the realisation that if they got into open wounds, they could kill.

When he started to encourage doctors to wash their hands, the rate of deaths in his wards plummeted. Previously, doctors had been operating on numerous people in their ward, not washing their hands in-between and so transferring germs between people with open wounds. It seems crazy, because hand washing is such a common feature of hospitals now (and life, really) that we totally take it for granted. But Semmelweis was the first to discover the need for it.

His crusade to reduce the number of deaths in his hospital is an awesome example of really trying to understand why a problem exists.

What makes this story even more interesting, though, is that outside of his hospital, other doctors didn't listen to him. They were offended that he thought that their dirty hands had been the problem all along. It was years after his death that hand washing finally caught on in other hospitals.

Perhaps as educators we are too quick to rule out the possibility we might be one of the reasons the problems exists? If we took responsibility more often for the mistakes we might be making, we could solve problems faster! (Remember the old adage: 'Every time you point at someone, there are three fingers pointing back at you!')

This willingness to take responsibility is perfectly summed up by a guy called Benjamin Zander, who is a conductor in Boston. If his orchestra is not playing well, he asks *himself* the question, 'Who am I being, that the sparks around me are dying away, a flame unrealised?'

If the fact that the other doctors didn't listen to Semmelweis makes you sad, don't worry. We are going to teach you how to solve problems like Dr Semmelweis and, perhaps more importantly, how to then share those solutions so that people adopt them and many, many lives are changed.

1. What am I passionate about?
2. We believe...
3. But right now the reality is...
4. **What are the root causes?**

So why does the problem keep happening?

So let's stick with our idea of 'We believe in a school where all teachers work together to achieve great results for all of our kids'.

If we asked you why this isn't happening in your school, you might say:

'We are just too busy.'

or,

'They don't care anymore.'

Chances are, you are wrong.

In innovation, we need to acknowledge our assumptions and go way deeper if we really want to understand the root causes of a problem.

Remember, Dr Semmelweis's early assumptions were, 'Children die if the mother doesn't give birth on her side' or 'Children die if the priest rings a bell'!

If you brought in the world's most expensive consulting companies, filled with MBA graduates from the world's elite universities, to help you solve your problems, they would do a few things, but the most important would be attempt to get to the 'root of the problem'. We are going to share some of their secrets with you.

The following little exercise is called the 'root cause tree', and it is a really effective tool to help you understand problems in your school.

To start, grab a piece of A3 paper and draw a picture of a tree, like the one overleaf.

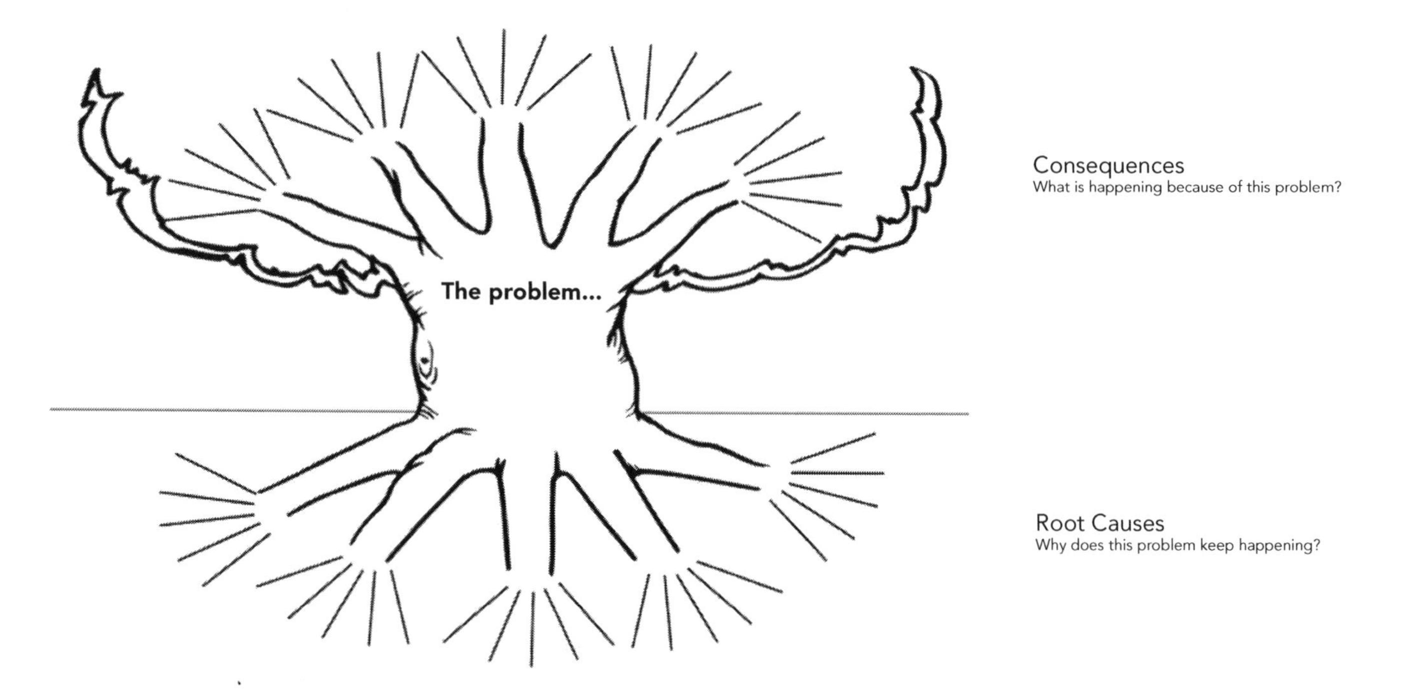
The problem...
Consequences
What is happening because of this problem?
Root Causes
Why does this problem keep happening?

The trunk

In the trunk of your tree, write the problem you are up against. Keep it really simple, something like:

'Kids aren't finding class time fun.'

or,

'Kids don't feel safe at school.'

or,

'Our teachers are not working together.'

or,

'Our parents are not engaged in the school.'

Again, the simpler the better here. As Winnie-the-Pooh said, 'It is more fun to talk with someone who doesn't use long, difficult words but rather short, easy words like "What about lunch?"'

The branches

In the branches of the tree, we need to detail the consequences of the problem. Let's go with the problem, 'Our teachers are not working together'.

What are some of the big things that happen as a result of this?

Maybe:

- more work for teachers
- a poor culture among the staff
- great ideas stay private
- no common practices and consistency
- lack of shared knowledge.

We write these consequences in the branches of the tree and then keep extending the branches out as we go a little further into each of them. What happens when there is more work for teachers? Maybe the teachers become burned out and their performance gets worse? Then maybe they leave the school and consistency gets even worse for the kids? Keep thinking about as many consequences as you can. What is happening because of this problem?

The more you understand the problem and its consequences, the more you can stick up for your idea. People might say, 'Sure, we'd like to get teachers working better together, but at the moment we all have a lot of work to do with these new curriculum changes and we can't get bogged down in new projects'.

'Aha!' you can then exclaim. 'I can help you with that!'

An understanding of the consequences of your problem is a good way to help get your immediate team on board, but it is a *great* tool for you to get your leadership and 'the system' on board.

See, the reality is that principals and system leaders are under constant pressure to address a whole range of issues, and priorities are ever changing, based on community pressure, political timing, or even the latest report from a university or think tank. If you are lucky, the focus of the day might align with the problem you are trying to solve... but let's not rely on luck.

Knowing the consequences that result from not addressing your problem is super important to these players. If you can go deep into the consequences and show alignment and wins for them, you might be able to get some traction and resources.

For example, if you are addressing student engagement, one of the consequences of not having engaged students is clearly poor learning outcomes. You can be pretty confident that addressing learning outcomes will always be important to parents, other teachers, the principal and the community. If you can show a direct correlation between improving student engagement and improving learning outcomes, you create a win–win for loads of people.

You can then take it a step further.

Student engagement in school can easily be shown to have benefits in reducing juvenile justice and health issues. Boom. You now have wins across different departments of government. The more you explore the consequences, the more wins you will find for others.

The more wins you find for others, the more help you will get. And the more people working on the problem, the better impact for the students.

By understanding your branches, you give yourself a massive leg up in making the change you want to see.

The roots

Now we understand the consequences better, let's go into the root causes.

Continuing with our problem that 'Our teachers are not working together', if we were to dig down into the root causes of this we may determine some big reasons teachers are not attending planning meetings regularly. These might include:

- they are too busy
- their schedules don't match up
- staff don't get along
- planning together has not been fun before
- we don't know each other's strengths.

We then write these into the big roots on our tree. (In a few pages, we show you how to dig down further into each of these root causes to find deeper causes.)

To see what a nice root cause analysis tree looks like, check overleaf.

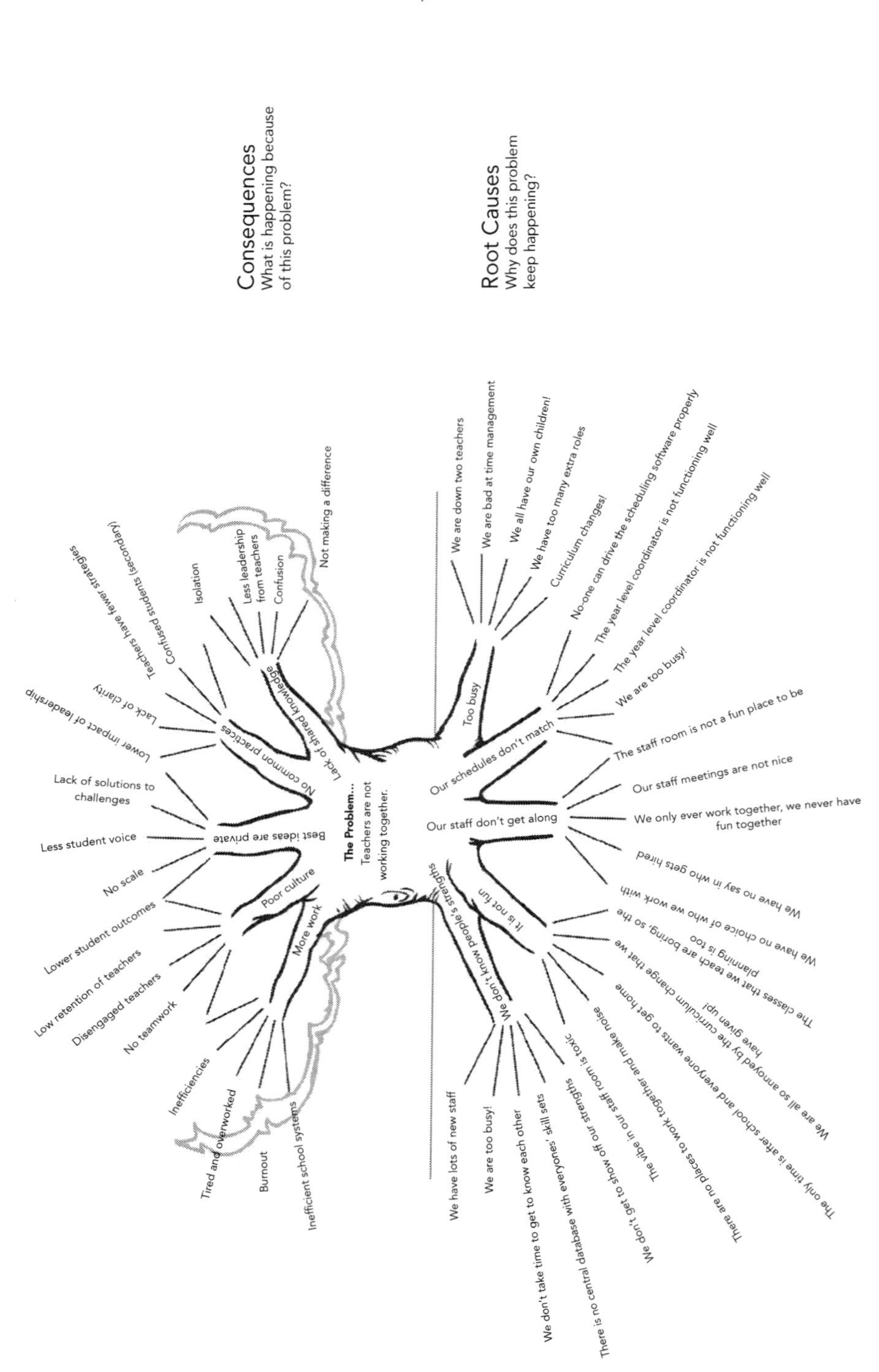
Consequences
What is happening because of this problem?
Root Causes
Why does this problem keep happening?
The Problem...
Teachers are not working together.
Lack of shared knowledge
No common practices
Best ideas are private
Poor culture
More work
Isolation
Less leadership from teachers
Confusion
Not making a difference
Confused students (secondary)
Teachers have fewer strategies
Lack of clarity
Lower impact of leadership
Lack of solutions to challenges
Less student voice
No scale
Lower student outcomes
Low retention of teachers
Disengaged teachers
No teamwork
Inefficiencies
Tired and overworked
Burnout
Inefficient school systems
Too busy
Our schedules don't match
Our staff don't get along
It is not fun
We don't know people's strengths
We are down two teachers
We are bad at time management
We all have our own children!
We have too many extra roles
Curriculum changes!
No-one can drive the scheduling software properly
The year level coordinator is not functioning well
The year level coordinator is not functioning well
We are too busy!
The staff room is not a fun place to be
Our staff meetings are not nice
We only ever work together, we never have fun together
We have no say in who gets hired
We have no choice of who we work with
The classes that we teach are boring, so the planning is too
We are all so annoyed by the curriculum change that we have given up!
The only time is after school and everyone wants to get home
There are no places to work together and make noise
The vibe in our staff room is toxic
We don't get to show off our strengths
There is no central database with everyones' skill sets
We don't take time to get to know each other
We are too busy!
We have lots of new staff

Listen

Watch, and

understand

But this is all just speculation!

Yes!

Welcome to design thinking (which we have stripped down to its basics to keep things simple!).

At first, we need to make some educated assumptions.

Just try to fill your root cause tree as best you can with what you think is happening.

You can make your entries on this tree far more well informed, however, if you really start to ask your users some questions.

Try sitting down with some of your students, for example, and asking them why they don't see a purpose in school.

You might be fascinated by what they tell you.

Dig deeper (and listen to people … sort of)

Once we have the big root causes of our problem, it is then important to go deeper into our understanding of them.

The easiest way to do this is, once again, to ask yourself *why* a few times. Get as deep as you can into the root causes of your problem.

For example, if we were looking at the problem 'Kids are not engaged', a root cause might be:

'The kids don't see the purpose of the school.'

Why?

'Because they don't have good role models in the community.'

Why?

'Because kids who do well leave the town and don't come back to engage with the school.'

Why?

'Because they are embarrassed by the school.'

Why?

'Because we have never tried to build a legacy of success in the school.'

(After a while it gets annoying, kind of like Macaulay Culkin in *Uncle Buck*, but you get the idea.)

This would put us five roots deep. If we do this for all of the roots, chances are we would be really starting to understand the problem we wrote on our trunk.

Let's imagine we are talking to a kid that doesn't like maths. Try the five *whys* technique. For example:

'Why don't you like maths?'

'Because it is boring.'

'Why is it boring?'

'Because I don't get it.'

'Why don't you get it?'

'Because I get confused in class.'

'Why do you get confused in class?'

'Because I don't understand things in class, and then I try to do them for homework and I get them wrong.'

'Why do you not understand things in class?'

'Because the teacher moves too fast for me and I am scared to ask for help because the other kids laugh at me.'

Okay. Now we are getting somewhere. We could dig deeper into this and perhaps find that the key issue is a textbook one, or a classroom management one, or it could be how we are differentiating, or doing group work.

Another tip when looking for root causes and deeper causes is to listen to people, but watch them as well (in a non-creepy kind of way). You are often getting insights here, more than you are getting ideas, and it is unlikely that your users will tell you exactly the solution that they need.

As Henry Ford said, 'If I had asked people what they wanted, they would have said faster horses'.

Maybe just take your coffee and a notepad outside one day to see what kids do as they walk into the school. Or ask a teacher to sit at the front of a maths class to watch the facial expressions of kids as a new topic is introduced.

You could ask your students to jot down in a notebook, on a scale of one to ten, how happy or how tired they are at each hour of the day.

Or maybe don't think about asking what they do, but why they do it.

Or you could try to put yourself in their shoes.

In their book *Creative Confidence*, David and Tom Kelley write about the young doctor who faked an ankle injury and then had a camera in his hat that recorded everything he saw during his hours in the emergency ward. (Turns out his entire view was looking up at a dull roof, with the occasional person reaching over him.) The Kelleys point out, 'Behaviours are never wrong to design thinkers, but they are meaningful'.

This is all about empathy here. The more you can understand the experience of the person you are trying to solve a problem for, the better your solution will be.

1. What am I passionate about?
2. We believe...
3. But right now the reality is...
4. What are the root causes?
5. Other players?

You will not solve this problem alone

So, maybe we have built up your ego a little by now.

But just as you were preparing to tackle this problem single-handedly and become the next Sal Kahn of the education sector, we have another little secret to let you in on.

You will not solve this problem alone.

Chances are, a huge number of books, non-profits, reports, websites, blogs, conferences, PhD students and companies are already trying to solve the same problem you have identified.

Spend a bit of time trying to identify as many of these players as you can. Who else is working in this space?

You don't need to fight with these guys; instead, you should be friends with them! They might be able to help you, or give you some great ideas. Innovation is not always about creating new things. Sometimes you can copy what is already working somewhere else, adapt the ideas to new situations, or collaborate with other players to get a better outcome.

1. What am I passionate about?
2. We believe...
3. But right now the reality is...
4. What are the root causes?
5. Other players?
6. **Focus on one root cause.**

Picking just one root

As mentioned, Aaron led an HIV/AIDS orphanage in Makuyu, a small village in Kenya, for a year. While there, his team was trying to tackle a whole raft of challenges in the community.

They did many root cause analysis trees during their time there, but one of the tougher ones was where they wrote in the trunk, 'Girls are skipping and dropping out of school'. The consequences of this problem were heartbreaking, with many girls falling pregnant, contracting STIs, remaining trapped in poverty and dying young.

For months Aaron and his team tried to understand this problem. They chatted with parents, teachers, the girls, their boyfriends and anyone else they could think of to try to get a deeper understanding of what was going on. There were all sorts of root causes: the need for the girls to work on the farm, the lack of educated female role models, the fact that school was boring and the feeling among parents that they couldn't afford to invest in the girls.

One day they were chatting to the girls again and Aaron asked, 'How many days a month do you usually miss?' When they blushed and said timidly, 'Around five', Aaron decided to leave the conversation and let Kaitlin take over.

It turned out that every time they had their period, they skipped class.

While this problem is now commonly recognised in education in very poor communities, back then it was the first that Aaron and Kaitlin had heard of it. When they looked at the massive root cause tree they had drawn on a wall with chalk, with around a hundred different roots coming down from the trunk, they put a big circle around this particular issue. They figured if they could get rid of this root cause, they could take a big step closer to solving the problem of girls dropping out of school.

So now that we understand the root causes of your problem, and who some of the other players are, we need to pick one of the root causes we want to chop at.

Let's imagine we take a step back and look at our tree. We hate that tree. With the problem spray-painted on the trunk and all the horrible consequences on the branches, we really want this tree to die. (Bear with us on this metaphor, greenies, we don't usually like killing trees, just these bad ones!) But what usually happens in schools is that we just snip away at the consequences (the branches) rather than getting down to the roots. This is almost always the wrong approach.

Now imagine that we invite a whole load of great people who are trying to solve this problem over to our backyard. They don't like this tree either. We give each of them a shovel and an axe. They look at all the root causes and start to decide which one they are most qualified to chop at (and the one they really want to chop at).

Once you see what roots other people are chopping at, you need to decide which one you want to chop at.

Every now and then you might help someone else on their root, but the reality is, the best job you can do is chop through the one root that you are focused on.

It is this refined and well-understood root cause you have identified that we are now going to try to solve.

We have just found our clog-wearing French farmers who are grumpy about their feet getting muddy and wet because their wooden shoes are not up to the task.

The root cause we are going to focus on is...
(finish the sentence)

Check-in

So we are powering through this Changemaker Journey! We have statements for the following:

'We believe in a school where...'

'But right now the reality is...'

'The root cause we are trying to solve is...'

If you can confidently fill in these three sentences, you have the foundation you need.

You have a dream of a new future for your school. And you have taken the time to dig down to understand the problem you want to solve.

Now we get into the fun stuff.

Making.

Make

So, getting back to my original idea...

Earlier in the book, we talked about how when people come to us with an idea that they have had, we ask them to take a step back and understand the problem.

What sometimes happens is that they come back with a better understanding of the problem they are trying to solve and then say, 'So, getting back to my original idea...' At which point (probably to their great frustration), we interrupt them again.

Because the reality is, the first idea is often the worst idea.

Remember that innovation is not about trying to squash your solution into problems; instead, it's about starting with a problem and then solving that.

So this idea you have in your head might be good.

Chances are, though, that the forty-seventh idea might just be the best one. We are going to teach you some simple and powerful skills that will help you to quickly come up with many more solutions to your root cause. Some of them might be crazy and never see the light of day, but the more ideas we come up with here, the greater the chances of us stumbling upon that brilliant solution that changes the game for many, many kids.

The school of hard knocks

You might remember that earlier on we mentioned that Aaron received 'a handful of pretty serious death threats' when he was running a school in Tanzania.

What might surprise you is that these death threats didn't come from local gangsters or religious extremists.

They came from kids in the school. The very kids he was working so hard for.

One afternoon, when they had been at the school for six months, Aaron was marking some papers in his little shack in the slum. One of the teachers, who we will call Anthony, walked past (he was the only one left actually, as the others had been fired or had decided to leave). Aaron asked Anthony to pop in and share a cup of tea, hoping to inspire him with a little pep talk. He was a brilliant teacher—a local guy who had grown up tough but had made it through school and wanted to help the next generation. All of the teachers had been doing it tough, trying to teach 200 kids, with almost no budget, living among crime and hardship, and constantly trying to overcome new bouts of malaria.

As Aaron made a tea for Anthony, he started to talk.

'You have been amazing, my friend, and I feel like we are really making progress here', Aaron said as he lit the small gas stove to boil some water. 'I know things are tough, but I feel like if we can just push that little bit harder this month, the kids will see the progress they are making and we will be on track to getting a load of them through their exams'.

'Aaron, you need to take a break', Anthony said, slumping into a chair.

'I didn't come to this place to take breaks', Aaron said, without turning around, putting a teabag into each mug and spoonfuls of sugar into Anthony's tea. 'I came here to work with awesome people like you, man, and to make a difference for these kids.'

'No, Aaron, honestly,' he said. 'You need to get away.'

Aaron turned around and smiled. 'Anthony, we can do this. We are going to get ten of these kids through these exams this year and prove to the whole community that this school changes lives.'

Anthony put up his hand to interrupt.

'Aaron, you are not listening. You must get away.' Fear was etched on his face. Then he looked down. 'I overheard some of the boys talking about you at break.'

'Cool—what are they saying?' Aaron asked. 'Let's fix it and move on.'

'Aaron, it's really bad,' Anthony responded. 'In a few hours the boys are going to come to your house and, in front of Kaitlin, they are going to kill you.'

This stopped Aaron in his tracks. This was real, very real, and this was not the kind of place where the police could come to the rescue or a counsellor could be called in from head office. There were no protocols here for something like this.

Remember that quote from Nietzsche, 'He who has a why to live by can bear almost any how'? For Aaron, the kids at the school were the *why*. They were the reason he had been pushing through all the struggles in the school. But now some of them wanted him dead?

As an officer in the military, Aaron had worked hard to look after the men he led. He would go in to fight for them and he felt he had their respect. But here, at this school, he had failed as a leader—failed like he had never failed before. As Anthony talked to him, almost every voice in his head told him to quit—then and there—and then pack up his bags and leave this incredibly difficult place. He didn't know if he was willing to die in this place, for these kids. He didn't know if his *why* was that strong.

But he had a little bit of commitment left in him and he decided to do something. And he knew that he had to do it quickly.

Aaron told Anthony to ask Kaitlin into the house as soon as school finished. Giving her a kiss on the cheek as he passed her, he then found one of the student leaders and asked him to gather as many of the boys as he could and meet him in one of the classrooms.

Then he went into the class and sat down to wait. As the boys streamed in, many of them his age, he glanced around at the posters they had put up together, showing quotes from leaders like Martin Luther King Jr, Nelson Mandela and Rosa Parks. In a few minutes, fifty of them were inside and he asked a boy at the back of the room to pull the door shut.

He stood up in front of them all, took a breath and said, 'The rumour is that you want to kill me tonight'. He then looked around the room, took a breath and threw them a challenge. 'Well, I don't want Kaitlin to see it happen, so try to kill me right now.'

Then he waited for them to run at him.

But none of them moved.

He challenged them again, saying 'Come on! We talk about being men of courage, men of honour; let's do this thing!'

He fully expected them to rush at him. But still none of them moved.

And at that moment he knew that he had it all wrong.

He had come to that slum to fix it. He was convinced that he had the answers to change the school. He felt that if he could lead that school with everything he had, never giving up on the kids, their futures could change. But it hadn't worked, and he had screwed up badly. With tears in his eyes he took another breath and said, '*Pole sana*. I am so sorry'.

In the school they could only afford one stick of chalk each week, but this time he gave it to them, and asked them to tell him everything that he had done wrong. He sat on the side of the room, and they proceeded to tell him his failures ... for three hours.

At the core of it all, though, was a very simple message: 'Aaron, all of this stuff is your vision, not ours'.

This was really tough for him to hear. Together with Kaitlin, he had seen how little hope was in the school when they had arrived six months earlier. The boys in that room knew what the future looked like for them if they didn't get an education—and it wasn't pretty. Then he asked them what their vision was for the school. They rewrote their personal and collective visions on the board that day, setting bigger goals and harder rules for themselves than Aaron and Kaitlin had set. Kaitlin did the same thing with the girls later that night.

Aaron realised that change wasn't going to come from him. Change had to come from the people who wanted change more than he could ever want change in that place.

That day, he learned one of the most powerful and valuable lessons of his life—that the only thing more powerful than ownership is authorship.

So often as leaders we write the plan, and then slide it across the table to our team, hope they take ownership of it, and get frustrated when they don't. We say, let your team write the plan, and develop their own solutions. Then they will really own them.

The only thing more powerful than ownership is authorship.

Working together

So there is a *very small* chance you can do all this on your own.

Maybe you can be the inspiring, revolutionary founder who wins all the prizes and gives the speeches.

But it is whole lot more fun, and a great deal easier, to do it with others.

And doing it yourself is like one hand clapping. You get tired quickly and you don't make a lot of noise. As Helen Keller said, 'Alone we can do so little. Together we can do so much'.

So work with people here. It doesn't matter what you call them. They could be your 'professional learning community', your 'school improvement subcommittee' or your 'edupreneurship team'. Bring together a group of people, including kids and parents, who are passionate about making your school better, and use these tools to solve problems.

If you like, you can all use this process to focus on individual things that each person in your group identifies they care about, or you can get all 'Captain Planet' on one problem and combine all your powers to solve one root cause. Your call.

Going alone is like clapping with one hand.

Creating a space for innovation

As a school principal, Dave would wake up early and get some coffee (or Red Bull) into his blood to kickstart his brain. Then he would open his diary to try to determine what fires he needed to put out that day.

There was that lesson to observe, the conversation to have, the emails to write, the inbox to clear, the strategy to finalise, the visit from head office, the staff member who was going through a bad patch, the call to the police station to chat about a kid who was in trouble, an event to organise and the school council meeting to run. At around 7 pm he would drive home, exhausted but satisfied, feeling like he had done his best to make a difference that day.

Trouble was, Dave often felt like he was being reactionary rather than revolutionary in his leadership. He loved strategy and innovation, and wished that he could spend more time leading in this way rather than constantly responding.

One day he tried to do things differently, deciding to focus more of his time on ensuring that his team had a feeling of authorship and autonomy in their work. He started to encourage them to solve problems and come up with ways to make the school better. Often he found the simpler their ideas, the better thought out they were. He committed to saying yes as much as he could.

Our good friend Peter Hutton, an inspiring school leader at Templestowe College in Melbourne, Australia, has a pretty cool way of encouraging innovation in his school. A couple of days a week, coffee in hand, he sits in the main common area of his school with a little sign that says, 'Ideas will be approved quickly'. He then waits to see which staff and students walk up to him with a concept that he can quickly sign off on. Nice idea, Peter!

What you need

On a scale of one to ten, how innovative do you think your school is? (By the way, if it is a ten, let us know—we want to come and check it out!)

If your school needs to be more innovative, where do you start? By asking people to brainstorm at staff meetings? Or by setting up an 'innovation sub-committee' to report on findings in three months' time? (Usually the two most common approaches we see, by the way!)

People in the sector will try to convince you that too many complexities exist in education to make schools innovative. We disagree. Helping to make a school more innovative is simple. Create an environment where people are comfortable being creative.

This doesn't necessarily mean that you need to be like Google and have sleeping pods, colourful bean bags, slides in your lobby and free food. Creating amazing learning environments is nice but not absolutely necessary—or, as Aaron's wife said to him once, 'It doesn't matter what teapot you have, you just need to make good tea'.

We know that in schools, we don't have quite the same budget as Google, so we need to do things a little leaner. But don't fear, we have had teams of edupreneurs use these super-cheap innovation tools all around the world—from elite private schools to township schools in slums—and they consistently get awesome results.

Here is what you need:

- *The five tools in the next few pages:* They are super simple, easy to teach to your team and, we think, massively effective!
- *A team:* Around five people is perfect. The more diverse the better (and try to include some of the people who you are solving a problem for).

- *Paper:* Sticky notes are great, but if you can't find them or afford them, just rip up some paper into small squares (around 8 cm by 8 cm).
- *Pens:* One for each person.
- *Feet:* People think better (and there is much better energy) if people ideate while they are standing up.
- *Music:* Play some music! Have fun! Music is scientifically proven to make people more creative.

Depending on how innovative your team is, the ideas in the coming pages may be pretty different from what you are used to.

1. What am I passionate about?

2. We believe...

3. But right now the reality is...

4. What are the root causes?

5. Other players?

6. Focus on one root cause.

7. Ideate fifty solutions.

Tool 1: Lots of ideas please

Tool number one is to come up with lots of ideas to solve your root cause. (We often say that you and your team should come up with at least a hundred.) This does not take as long as you might think, and if your team is powering along you can do it easily in thirty minutes.

So in your ideation session, get everyone standing up with a handful of sticky notes each and some pens.

Put some tunes on.

Then start coming up with ideas to solve your root cause.

Every time someone has an idea, they should write it on a sticky note or a piece of paper, and then say it out loud as they put it down in the middle of the table.

The team at design and consulting firm IDEO are the most vocal and famous advocates for coming up with a quantity of ideas. When throwing a hundred solutions at a problem, they found that ideas number one to sixty gave them some interesting results. Ideas sixty to eighty often got pretty crazy, as the team was pushing their creativity. But between ideas eighty and one hundred there were often around six brilliant ideas that they wanted to move forward with. As we said before, first idea, worst idea, so commit in your ideation session to trying to come up with at least a hundred solutions to your root cause.

So let's say we are trying to come up with ideas to better engage parents in our school. To solve this root cause, we might start ideating with the following:

1. Let's offer free coffee at our parent–teacher events!
2. Let's change our parent–teacher events to Saturday mornings!
3. Let's put on a moonlight cinema movie night and do meetings with parents before the movie starts!

So we are already at three ideas — only ninety-seven to go!

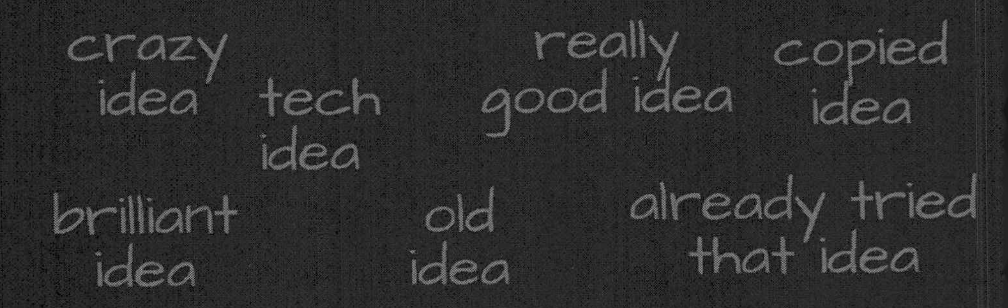

IDEA WALL

okay idea

outrageous idea

rude idea

idea from Sarah

funny idea

expensive idea

new idea

Tool 2: Crazy ideas allowed (and encouraged)

Our second tool of ideating is that we *encourage crazy ideas.*

Nothing is sacred in the ideation phase and crazy ideas are fine.

So let's check in with our parent–teacher night. If we were open to getting more creative, we might suggest things like:

4 Let's pick them up in limousines to bring them to parent–teacher night!

5 Let's kidnap their children and only give them back once they have come in to meet us!

6 Let's give espresso shots and puppies to all the kids whose parents don't check in with teachers!

All of this is fine. If a negative thought came into your head when you were reading one of these, you need to train yourself to think in a different way if you are going to become an edupreneur!

So why do we encourage ridiculous ideas? Because sometimes they actually are pretty great!

At the moment Google is trying to get wi-fi to the entire planet, and the solution they are rolling out is floating hot air balloons over the surface of the earth. Pretty ridiculous, right?

But imagine 140 or so years ago when Alexander Graham Bell told people about the phone. 'So, if you talk into one receiver that is connected to another receiver you can speak to each other even if you are not in the same room. And if we just connect every one of these receivers to every other receiver with billions of miles of cables we will all be able to talk to each other whenever we want.' Might have seemed a little crazy, but humanity did it.

We didn't think we needed iPads until Steve Jobs made us fall in love with them.

The architect for Sydney's Opera House resigned during the build because his ideas were too out there and conflicted with the state government of the day, but they eventually finished building the thing and it has become world famous.

We were working with a group of fourteen-year-olds and we asked them, 'How could every kid eat healthy food every day in your school?' After hearing about air-dropped smoothies, and swimming pools full of salad, one kid yelled, 'Let's rip out all of the trees and plant fruit trees!' If you walk around their school now, you can grab an apple straight from the tree. Pretty cool.

Every time someone is negative about an idea, they kill the creativity in the group.

So any idea offered during the ideation phase is cool. Just get them down and keep moving towards one hundred solutions.

Look among the craziest ideas to find the genius.

Tool 3: Yes, and…

The reason we encourage lots of crazy ideas is that we don't know where they might go.

So tool three is that we say, 'Yes, and'—an idea that was made famous by the comic geniuses from Second City (and recently written about in depth by Second City executives Kelly Leonard and Tom Yorton).

The idea here is that one idea sparks another idea.

Let's check in once more with our first three parent engagement ideas:

1. Let's offer free coffee at our parent–teacher events.
2. Let's change our parent–teacher events to Saturday mornings.
3. Let's put on a moonlight cinema movie night and do meetings with parents before the movie starts.

Someone might then say:

'Yes, and

7. We could do the movie night on a Friday because the parents need to come in anyway to pick up their kids,

and,

8. Give the parents a glass of wine instead of a coffee so it is more fun.'

Okay, now this is sounding like a parent–teacher night that more people might want to get involved with!

Let's keep going—we are at eight ideas now and only ninety-two to go before we get to one hundred!

'Wacky idea but what if we…'

↓

'Hey, that is interesting actually; what if we…'

↓

'Ooh, I like that and maybe we could also…'

↓

'Brilliant! You know that might just work. Great job team…'

Tool 4: 'We'

What?! 'Give the parents alcohol at school?!' We can't do that!

Did that jump into your head when you read idea eight—'give the parents a glass of wine instead of a coffee so it is more fun'. If so, we still have work to do, friends!

We are going to keep the negativity away with our fourth tool, which is using the following line:

'We need to think about that.'

This keeps you working together. So if you are worried about plying parents with wine to get them to come along to the parent–teacher night, raise your concern, but do it in a way similar to the following:

> 'Hey, I love the idea about the parents getting glasses of wine at the moonlight cinema, but we could also think about some non-alcoholic drinks to set a good example?
>
> *'What if we*
>
> 9 Still served the drinks and had some of the teachers running a separate babysitting club for the kids while the parents watched their movie?'

This could then be followed by, 'Yes, and we could

10 Serve really tasty iced tea instead of wine!'

Or let's imagine idea number eleven was 'Let's strap GoPro cameras to all the kids so the parents can see what they get up to all day.' And then someone might add, 'We need to think about a way to do that cheaply because those GoPros are pretty pricey', which makes someone else jump in with idea number twelve: 'We could just have one GoPro per class and every month a video cycles around the class.'

Only eighty-eight more ideas to go!

Clear out the bad vibes and squishy faces.

Tool 5: It's all good

And the final tool in the ideation kit is that all ideas are good. (This is similar to the second tool, but here we focus specifically on removing negativity.)

Again, anyone who is shutting ideas down is destroying the creativity in the room and we need everyone's ideas. As they say at IDEO, a lot of us are smarter than any of us.

We all know that in many staff rooms we have the people we like to call 'happiness vacuums'. They just seem to come into a room and suck the life out of it! If they keep doing it, you need to figure out a way to turn their negativity into positivity (or, if that doesn't work, just a way to keep them quiet!).

We keep things positive by writing everyone's name on a piece of paper and sticking it to the wall. We then give a 'negative pen' to one person in the room (sometimes the most negative one!) and tell them that every time someone shuts down an idea, moans or even squishes their face up they get chalked up — and each mark means they owe a dollar to the Friday drinks kitty.

If you use this, or something similar, people will quickly figure out it is expensive to stay negative in your team!

'There are no rules here. We're trying to accomplish something.'

Thomas Edison

Copy, collaborate
and create
your way to an
awesome solution.

Imitation is the best form of flattery

Still can't get to one hundred ideas with these tools?

The reality is some super cool stuff is already happening out there. You don't necessarily have to create something from scratch.

Have a look at what other people are up to. What is working in your own school? In other schools? Other cities? Spend a bit of time searching online to see if fun things are happening that you didn't know about. Maybe put up a post on Facebook or tweet around a bit to see if people can alert you to cool things that are out there (throw #educhange in there to tap into the EC tribe).

Before you think about creating something new, see what you can copy or adapt, or who you can collaborate with.

Chances are, if you can help someone grow their idea by bringing it to your school, they are going to be very happy about it! Also, if you can outsource all of the hard work by buying something off the shelf (say, a great app or piece of software or a training program) you are going to get to where you need to go quicker and often cheaper.

As we always say, imitation is the best form of flattery (actually, to be fair, Charles Caleb Colton said that first).

Of course, if you want to copy an idea, use your best judgement to decide whether you need to ask the creator's permission to do so, and try your best to acknowledge them.

Picking a winner

So you have come up with one hundred ideas.

Now is the time to focus down onto just two of them. Let's jump back to our parent engagement idea.

We might drop number five ('Let's kidnap their children and only give them back once they have come in to meet us!') because, frankly, think of how much time we would have to waste in the courts trying to solve that mess. But our parent–teacher, moonlight cinema idea was looking interesting.

Also (even though we said, 'First idea, worst idea') maybe this time our very first idea of offering coffee to parents might actually be cool.

What if we set up a coffee cart in the car park or close to the school's entrance so when parents dropped off their kids they could grab a coffee and chat with teachers?

So we have our moonlight cinema idea, and our coffee cart idea.

Both are cool. Or so we think.

But chances are they both might suck. So we need to get to work figuring out if they are going to be a success or a flop.

We need to see if other people think they are cool as well. In other words, we need to bake reality into them quickly.

Let's move ahead with these two ideas and put the rest of them on the backburner.

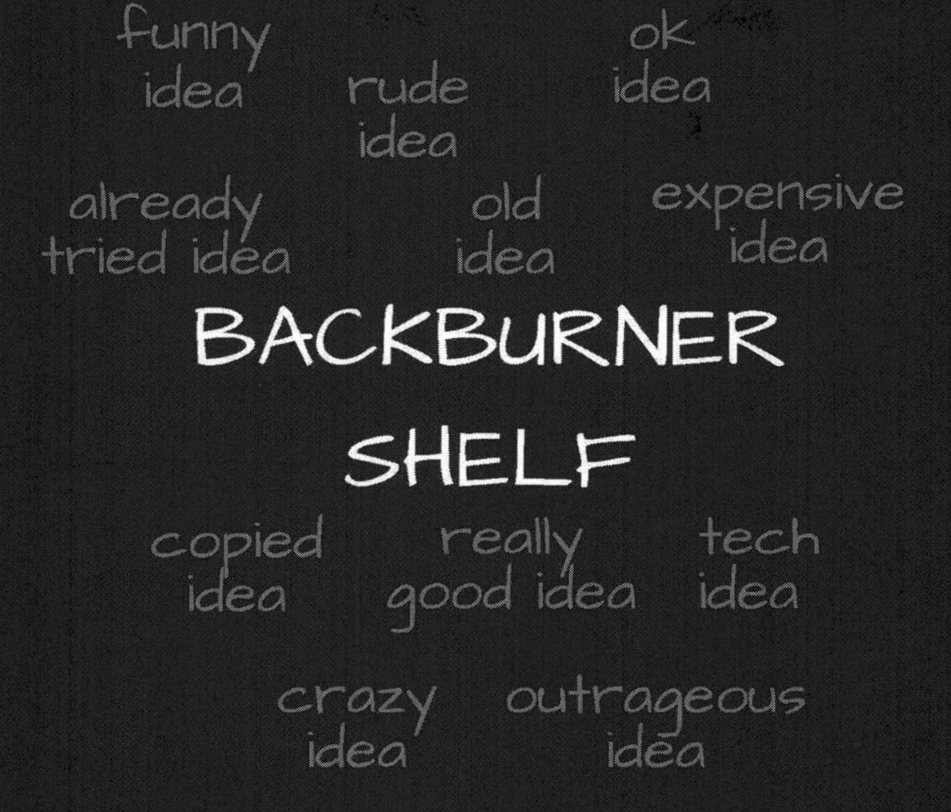

New idea   Brilliant idea

TEST SHELF

Watermelon juice

(Here we give you a quick business concept from Aaron.)

A couple of years back I was in Indonesia for a holiday. I was super relaxed after spending a week with my family in the sun, eating tasty food and reading books.

Every morning while I was there, I would wake up and stroll down to a little *warung* (roadside cafe) where I would order an omelette and a fresh watermelon juice. Drinking that cold juice, on a humid morning in the tropics, was heaven.

I started to wonder whether I could have this joyous juice experience back home and realised that no-one was selling juice like this. Would people back home enjoy watermelon juice as much as I did, if I made it available to them? I wondered whether an awesome business idea could be at play here.

As is usual for me on holidays, I got out a notebook and started playing with an idea. I realised I could go about launching my watermelon juice company in two ways.

Firstly, if I wanted to go the old-fashioned business route, I could spend a few months writing up a hundred-page business plan that detailed how I saw my watermelon juice company growing, and making lots of money. Once I was armed with this business plan, I would go out and find some investors who believed in me and my idea enough to throw a few million bucks my way to hire a team and get my company up and running.

Then I would spend the next year talking with branding companies so my bottles looked great, setting up my bottling plant, organising my watermelon suppliers, coordinating the trucks to deliver my bottles to shelves and trying to secure some big contracts so that I could start selling in supermarkets. All the while I would be chewing through money, and hoping like hell that my idea was going to work.

Or, secondly, I could try another approach. Drawing upon 'lean startup' principles made famous by Eric Ries and Steve Blank, I could figure out a quick and cheap test to see if my idea was any good or not.

So on the first Saturday after returning from Bali, I would head to the store early that morning to buy twenty watermelons, and then take my blender from home and set up a little store at my local markets. At my stall, I would put up a sign advertising 'Aaron's Wonderful Watermelon Juice, $5'.

If I sold out in an hour, then I would know I was onto something awesome. I should persevere with the idea and maybe one day I could grow my watermelon juice company into a big money maker.

If some people bought my juice, but commented that it could be sweeter, or they would like to take some home instead of drinking it fresh in the cup at the markets, I might consider making some tweaks.

If nobody bought my watermelon juice, I would know the idea was a flop. But it was a three-hour, $50 flop (the cost of my watermelons, which I could probably eat myself anyway, seeing as I loved watermelon juice so much).

See the difference between the two approaches? The first is high risk and it will take me a year or two to figure out if the idea is good. The second approach bakes (or juices) reality into my idea over a few hours at the Saturday markets. I know very quickly if my idea is good or bad.

(*Note:* I never did launch my little Watermelon Juice Company. On the plane home, I spilled milk on my jeans with the silly little milk containers they give you for your coffee and came up with another idea. With my 'milk ball' concept I was going to invent gelatinous balls that you could drop into your coffee on planes, which then dissolved the exterior skin so the milk could be mixed in.

No squirting of milk and no waste. Alas, I also remembered on the plane that back home I had a growing education social enterprise and a global non-profit to run, so both watermelon juice and milk balls were put on the backburner shelf.)

No more pilots

(And here Dave offers a quick interpretation of Aaron's watermelon juice idea.)

One of my jobs in this partnership is to help educators make sense of Aaron's sometimes crazy ideas. So let's look at his watermelon juice idea, and put it in an education setting. When I was a principal we were having huge problems with behaviour. We tried to think of all the reasons these problems were happening, but the root cause we decided to focus on was that at lunchtime the kids were sneaking out of school across the road to buy junk food, because we didn't have a functioning school cafeteria. Even the smallest kids were having litres of soft drink each lunch time and large serves of French fries.

We wondered if giving them healthy food at school for breakfast and lunch would make a difference. So we set up a little experiment, paying a local cafe to make a healthy breakfast and healthy sandwiches for lunch for one class of kids for two weeks. Then we tracked the number of behaviour incidents for that class.

The old way of doing this would have been to set up a big expensive pilot program to improve our school cafeteria that took years to make happen and hundreds of thousands of dollars to fund. We might even have to wait a few years for the funding to be approved and also for a few other schools to get on board. Then, after a while, someone would come in to write up a report on how it all went. By that time, chances are a lot of the staff who had first thought of the project would have moved on.

So the way I tested our healthy food idea was in the same way we encourage our teachers to do things now—using quick and cheap tests to see if our assumptions were true.

This is pretty hard for the education system to come to grips with because we are so stuck in our ways. Using quick and cheap tests on students is something that people find difficult to grasp. I am a strong advocate for them, and feel that a quick test with kids to see if an idea flies is better than a long, slow one.

Getting results quickly means if we find that something doesn't work like we thought it would, we can quickly pivot to finding something that does. Obviously, when you are testing an idea with kids, you need to make sure you do a few things. You need to keep the following in mind:

1. Keep the kids safe, and ensure their learning is not going to be affected in a seriously negative way by this test.
2. Don't get their hopes up too much. You can do this by just testing something quietly, without heralding the results you're expecting and implying that this is the way things are going to be from now on.

But we can also do something even before we test our ideas with real users. In the coming pages, we will show you a couple of ways that you can prototype your ideas.

When we prototype an idea, we come up with a creative way to share an idea with people to get their quick reactions. So the logic of 'the only way to get big rewards is to take big risks' doesn't work in edupreneurship.

Rather than taking big gambles that take years to determine the success of, we want you to start thinking in terms of little bets—quick and low-risk tests that give you a rapid indication as to whether your idea sucks, or if it is awesome.

A little bet like figuring out if the kids are more or less engaged in class if they get to choose the music that is played when they are working on a task. Or whether you get more parents along to the parent–teacher meetings if you team them up with the school athletics carnival, and run both events on a Saturday.

From today, you need to stop thinking about pilots. Prototype and act small—while continuing to dream big.

If your school is suffering from change fatigue, make change faster, more exciting and sexy (even when we get fatigued by things that are fast, exciting and sexy, we still love them).

Every failure takes you one step closer to success.

Kill ideas quickly

As an edupreneur you will probably get really pumped up by ideas all the time. You may come up with an idea in a Tuesday ideation session, spend the next two days telling everyone about how amazing it is going to be and talking your way around any criticisms that people direct at you.

What you need to do is have the courage to kill the idea quickly.

If you go from being massively inspired about an idea on Monday to dropping it on Thursday, that is a great result. Better a few days of your time wasted than a few years!

If an idea stinks, it doesn't matter how many nice ribbons you tie around it trying to convince people it is great, it still stinks. Or put another way, as brand strategy consultant Stephen Denny said, 'If dogs don't like your dog food, the packaging doesn't matter'.

Don't get down on yourself if you have to kill off your idea. The next one might be better!

If the idea is still good but the timing is bad, feel free to put it on the backburner shelf. Sometimes you might pick it up again in a few months, and sometimes it will stay where it should be, on the backburner shelf.

1. What am I passionate about?

2. We believe...

3. But right now the reality is...

4. What are the root causes?

5. Other players?

6. Focus on one root cause.

7. Ideate fifty solutions.

8. Prototype the best two.

Prototyping tool 1: User profile

With a user profile we draw a quick cartoon of the student or person we are trying to reach with our idea. Then we describe them quickly and propose our solution. Here's a quick example.

The situation: Jonny is very disruptive in class. He loves to get attention from his buddies. If someone is working hard, he distracts them. If he doesn't get attention he will get louder. In fact, making noise is his favourite thing. His parents are frustrated that Jonny isn't learning and they are blaming you.

Our solution: We have a friend who plays in a punk band. After conducting a police check on him, we have hired him to teach Jonny the drums (paying him $15 an hour). Jonny only gets to go to drum class if he collects five quiet credits in a week.

The best way for people to give you feedback on this possible solution is to ask, 'What do you like about the idea and what do you wish we did differently?'

Prototype tool 2: Story board

You could show this story board to a few people (including some mothers) and then ask them what they like about the idea and what they wish you would do to improve it.

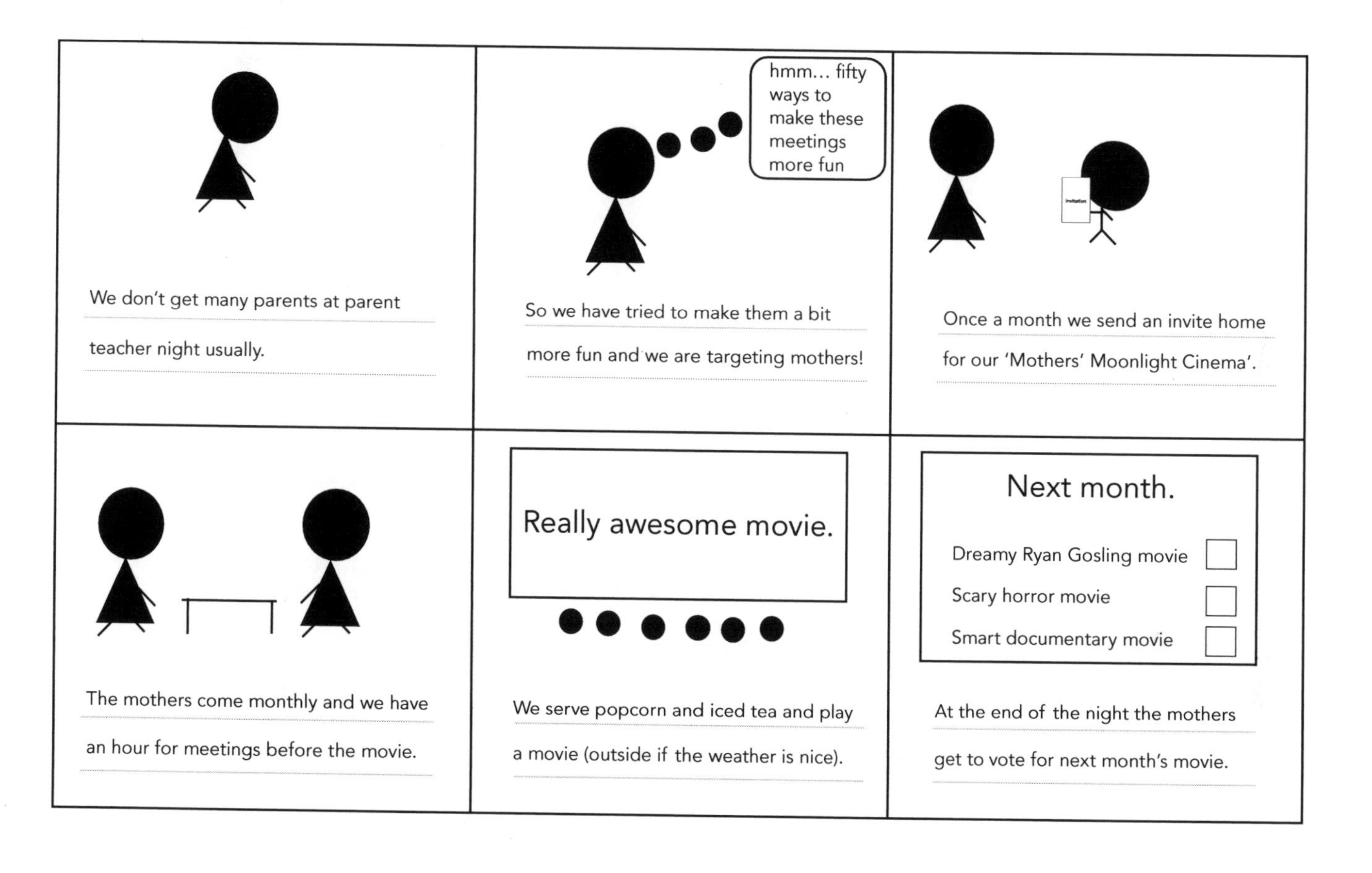
We don't get many parents at parent
teacher night usually.
hmm… fifty ways to make these meetings more fun
So we have tried to make them a bit
more fun and we are targeting mothers!
Once a month we send an invite home
for our 'Mothers' Moonlight Cinema'.
The mothers come monthly and we have
an hour for meetings before the movie.
Really awesome movie.
We serve popcorn and iced tea and play
a movie (outside if the weather is nice).
Next month.
Dreamy Ryan Gosling movie
Scary horror movie
Smart documentary movie
At the end of the night the mothers
get to vote for next month's movie.

Prototype tool 3: Miniature prototyping

A fun and quick way to get people to understand your idea is to build a little model of it.

You won't have to look far in the school to find some things to help you build your prototype.

Look for LEGO, pipe-cleaners, toilet rolls and cardboard. You can very cheaply and quickly piece together a model for people to have a glance at (see the example shown in the photo below).

Once again, when people get a glimpse of your idea in action ask them what they like about it and what they wish you would do to improve it.

Prototype tool 4: Physical prototyping

Another prototyping option is to create a life-size model of your idea.

Let's say you are prototyping your coffee van in the car park idea to get parents more engaged in the school. You want to run this idea by a handful of teachers and the parent council.

Grab a table and take it out to the car park. Get a piece of cardboard and write 'Free coffee for parents (and a free chat with teachers)' on it. Then have a few cookies and a few coffee mugs and run a few people through the experience as they walk into the school.

We know that teachers often don't like role-plays, but if you do have the guts to use this prototyping tool, you can get some great feedback really quickly.

Don't wait for perfect, just get started.

Leaving the laboratory

So you have all this cool feedback from your prototypes.

Now you need to decide which of your two ideas you think is best.

Before you get too excited, though, and think your best idea is amazing and going to rapidly solve your root cause and change the world, remember something very important.

Don't take this personally, but we still don't yet know if your idea is awesome, or if it sucks.

To test the idea further, we give it a quick working title (a name) and spend a bit of time fleshing it out.

For example, let's call our parent night Mothers' Moonlight Cinema.

We can very quickly determine that we will need a projector, some speakers, and a screen to help this night happen. We will also need food and drinks for the event. We can do it on the school sports field. We can market it with notes sent home with the kids. We can run it once a month.

But before we buy the projector and do all the marketing for the idea, we need to do a small test to see if the mums are going to come along or not! This idea does not need to be perfect (or perfectly worked out); we just need to give it a quick test to see what people think.

Going back to the watermelon juice idea, we are about to set up our little stall and see if this stuff sells!

1. What am I passionate about?
2. We believe...
3. But right now the reality is...
4. What are the root causes?
5. Other players?
6. Focus on one root cause.
7. Ideate fifty solutions.
8. Prototype the best two.
9. **Test the best.**

Testing time

So even though we think our Mothers' Moonlight Cinema is going to be a great way to encourage parents to engage with the school, we want to do a quick and cheap test.

How can we test this quickly and cheaply to see if it is going to make a difference?

Remember — this is not going to be a perfectly orchestrated event this first time. It is going to be a quick and cheap test.

Perhaps we just run it for one class?

We make it a nice little event.

We pop some popcorn (costing us $5), buy some plastic cups and make some tasty iced tea ($15).

We borrow a projector from the school and string up a bedsheet in a nice little grassy corner of the grounds.

Then the day before the event, we ask ourselves what an A+ result would look like, a B– and a Fail.

So for our Mothers' Moonlight Cinema maybe our grading system is:

A+ The mothers of twenty students come along. As a teacher, you are able to chat with most of them.

B– Eight mothers come along. You manage to get around to five of them before the movie starts.

F It is just you. With your popcorn and your iced tea and your strung up bedsheet, crying as you watch *Sleepless in Seattle*, ALONE.

1. What am I passionate about?

2. We believe...

3. But right now the reality is...

4. What are the root causes?

5. Other players?

6. Focus on one root cause.

7. Ideate fifty solutions.

8. Prototype the best two.

9. Test the best.

10. Pivot or persevere.

Pivot

So with the results of your test, and armed with the entrepreneurial terminology of Eric Ries and his lean startup ideas, you now need to decide whether to pivot or persevere.

So let's start with the 'F' result.

It was just you at the Mothers' Moonlight Cinema.

Sitting there with your popcorn and glass of iced tea and your strung up bedsheet, crying as you watched *Sleepless in Seattle*.

Alone.

This is where you need to pivot. It looks like this idea was a flop. Time to trial something else.

Maybe the coffee cart was better all along?

'I failed my way to success.'

Thomas Edison

The joy of failure

This page is for those who scored an F on their little test. (Well, all of you really, because if you are a true edupreneur you will score an F at some point.)

Don't take it personally.

Learn to love failure. Frame every failed test as 'one more thing we know isn't a solution to the root cause we are trying to solve'. After all, this is what we try to teach our students every day.

When Alexander Fleming was working to discover antibiotics he tried all sorts of things. He squeezed lemon juice in people's eyes (to then catch their tears, which contain lysozyme, a natural antiseptic). He even spent years trying to understand how chicken eggs didn't rot within hours of leaving a chicken.

He tried so many things and kept failing. One summer he left some petri dishes of cultures of staphylococci out, and mould started to grow in one dish. He came back after a two-week break and was blown away to see that the bacteria on the petri dish with the mould had been destroyed.

Penicillin was discovered.

Some would call it luck.

We say that you create your own luck.

You keep trying things until you figure out something, even by chance, that has the effect you were hoping for. Sometimes people say, 'How dare you test on children!' Our response is always that we would prefer a ten-minute test to a three-year pilot!

So if you need to pivot, don't worry. Bounce back, try something else, and who knows? Your penicillin could be just around the corner.

Persevere

Remember—at this stage, all you are doing is trying to figure out if you have an idea that makes a difference to the root cause you are trying to tackle.

So let's say the night was an A+ and the mothers of twenty students came along. As a teacher, you are able to chat with most of them. It looks like you have something pretty great on your hands here.

We would definitely recommend that you persevere with this idea, making it better and growing it into a regular offering in your school.

If it was a B– (eight mothers came along and you managed to get around to five of them before the movie started), then you could consider trying it again next month. Maybe you could improve your marketing approach, put on a different type of movie and think of other ways to get more mothers coming along? Maybe you have a longer time available for meetings with parents before the movie? Maybe you could target both parents?

This is still an idea to persevere with.

'I have more respect for the fellow with a single idea who gets there, than for the fellow with a thousand ideas who does nothing.'

Thomas Edison

Eureka!

If you scored an A+ or a B– on your test, well done.

But this is just the beginning.

Now it is time for you to turn your test into a really simple, clear product or a program that affects more than just one class of students.

We know how to get the change, now we need to go and make it happen for more kids.

This is what separates the doers from the talkers.

(And by the way, if you can't tell, we like hanging out with the doers.)

Share

My idea could make a difference:

beyond my class

beyond my school

beyond my country

Choose your own adventure

So, this is just the beginning.

In a business sense you have just made it through your startup phase, where you have worked hard to find a product that people will actually buy.

In an education sense, you have found something that affects the root cause like you hoped it would.

Awesome work.

Now you can move on to the point where you share your idea with many others. We need to turn this hunch, which has been backed up by a test, into something that can be rolled out beyond you to change the lives of many students. Entrepreneurs use the word 'product' to describe what they're developing, but as edupreneurs we use the word 'program'—a set of things that result in a similar outcome each time they are used.

So this is an exciting point to be at, but you are also at a very clear crossroads.

How far do you want to take this thing? Do you want to focus on affecting the kids in your school? Is that your 'Greensboro Four' moment?

Or do you want to have an impact on kids all around your town or city?

Or do you want to have an impact on kids around the world, seeing your idea making a difference in places you never thought it could?

Only you can answer these questions.

1. What am I passionate about?
2. We believe...
3. But right now the reality is...
4. What are the root causes?
5. Other players?
6. Focus on one root cause.
7. Ideate fifty solutions.
8. Prototype the best two.
9. Test the best.
10. Pivot or persevere.
11. **Turn the idea into something real.**

Think big,
act small.

Starting with your school

Even if you are aiming for a global impact with your idea, the best place to start to figure out how to grow your idea is in your school.

And the best way to start this shift is by turning your early idea into a clear program.

Let's look at a business example.

eBay

If we were trying to explain the eBay product to someone who is trying to sell something, we might say the following:

> eBay is a really easy way to go online and buy or sell items. If you want to sell an item, just create an account, upload a picture, give a brief description and then take your ad live. People can bid on your product until the auction ends (for a week or for another time period you specify). Once the winning bidder transfers funds for the product into your bank account, you can post it to them. (Another option is cash on pick up.) eBay usually takes just under a 10 per cent cut of the sale price. The address is ebay.com.

The eBay product might be a great solve for this person and they may use it.

You need to figure out exactly what your program does and what it does not do (we say that you should under-promise and over-deliver).

You could also try to condense your program to a one-page description, to explain to other teachers in your school how it works.

Or try to write it down like a recipe (like the example shown overleaf) so that other teachers can try it in their classes.

The **NAME** of our product: Mothers' Moonlight Cinema

The **NAMES** of our team members (including yours):
Margaret (Team Leader), Sarah (Events Manager), Theresa (Communications Leader), Janine (MC at Events)

The **PROBLEM** we are trying to solve: Our parent teacher nights are very unpopular with parents and as a result we have very little engagement with them throughout the year. There are lots of reasons why parents are not engaging with the school, but the root cause that we are trying to focus on is that our parent–teacher nights are not engaging, and parents don't find them enjoyable.

The **TEST** we conducted to determine this was worth pursuing:
We held a Mothers' Moonlight Cinema night with the mothers of the Year Five students last month on a Thursday. We put on some popcorn, some iced tea, and held an information session and question-and-answer session for ten minutes before we watched *Strictly Ballroom*. We usually have only five mothers at our parent teacher nights, but we had twelve along to the movie night. The mothers did a short survey and were asked if they 1) enjoyed the night, b) found it informative and c) would likely come back to another night. All of the mothers voted yes for every question, which was great. They gave some feedback and we now think we will change the night to Tuesday instead of Thursday, and also allow those mothers to book in a five-minute chat with the teacher before the movie starts. We are happy with the night and are persevering with the idea.

The **SPECIFICS** of our product (write it up like a recipe, it is the easiest way!):

- Every month we send out an email to all of the mothers at our school, inviting them to our Mothers' Moonlight Cinema which happens on the final Tuesday of every month.
- Mothers are able to book five-minute slots with their child's teacher using youcanbook.me
- On the night we start at 5:00, and meetings go through until 5:50.
- We then run a quick information and question-and-answer session for all of the mothers from 5:50 - 6:00.
- At 6:00 the movie starts (the mothers vote on the movie during the month by replying to the email). We set up in the school garden near the front office if it is nice, and in the basketball hall if it is rainy or cold.
- We have popcorn, cupcakes, iced tea and hot chocolate for sale during the night for a gold coin donation.
- At the end of the movie, mothers are able to leave questions or bits of advice on their seats, which helps the school to get better.

The **IMPACT** data we are hoping to collect:

- We are aiming for 90% of the students to have mothers who are actively engaged in the school and who attend at least three moonlight cinema events during the year.

Are you cool with this idea being posted on **ECIDEAS.ORG? (circle one)**
Yes No

Great ideas don't just take shape on their own—they are sculpted

Few people who achieve greatness simply have an idea and turn it into an instant hit.

Jim Carey would spend months preparing for his stand-up routines, testing out jokes and other bits at local comedy clubs to see what the audience found funny before he put it into his main routine.

Bob Dylan sometimes spent years writing one song, playing with different chords, lyrics and themes before it felt right.

Thomas Edison once famously said, 'I have not failed. I've just found 10 000 ways that won't work'.

At this stage of the process we are still learning things and have to work hard to make the program better as we go. Remember to stay green and growing with your idea!

Getting your principal on board

The most important person to keep on board at this point as you try to scale your program beyond your class is your principal. If they are on board, that is awesome for you. But if they decide to put a stop to your exciting idea, they can make things very difficult for you! If they are not on board, here is how you can try to change things (not in a manipulative way, but in a win–win kind of way).

First things first: you need to be a good operator. Imagine taking health tips from someone who smoked like a chimney and weighed over 130 kilograms! If you are not good at your job, your boss is unlikely to listen to your ideas.

Once you have sorted out if you are good at your job (or you have worked to get better), figure out ways to help your principal. Find out what their goals are, and the problems they are facing. If your idea can help them, they are going to be far more excited about it.

Always remember to time your requests. Principals are incredibly busy people, juggling many big responsibilities. You don't want to get a red light on growing your program just because you brought up a request at a busy time.

And finally, if your principal is driving you crazy and you are losing sleep about it, have an honest chat with them. If that doesn't work, stay professional and always try your best to do great work, even if coming to work each day is frustrating. Let your actions speak louder than your words and keep making a difference (and maybe start to look for either a promotion or another school in which to ply your edupreneurial brilliance).

Really awesome changes for lots of kids

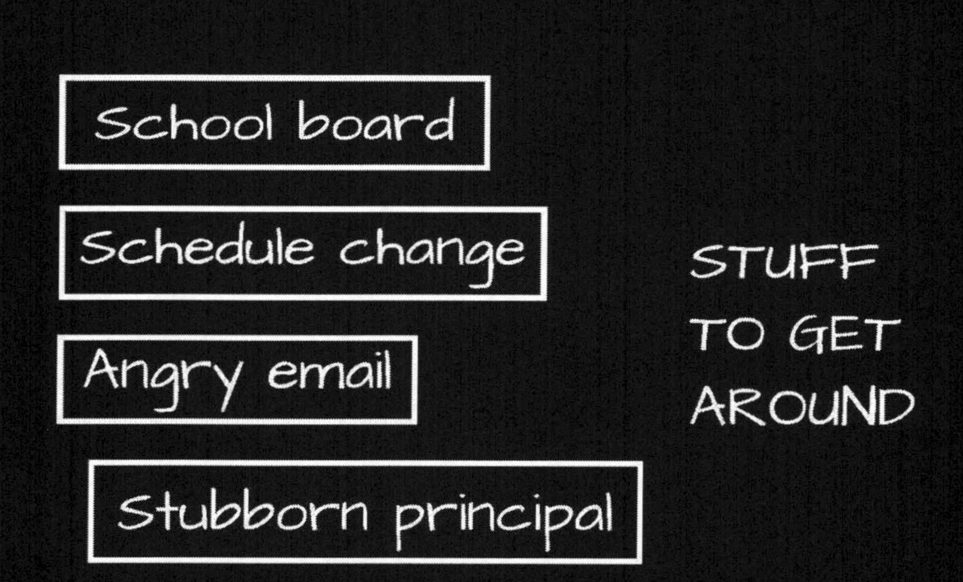

YOUR IDEA

'If you want to make enemies, try to change something.'

Woodrow Wilson

No way José

Now this is an important little section of the book that you must read carefully—before you get upset and send us a sad (or angry) email.

If you are challenging the status quo, you will upset people. You will be blocked and told no.

Deal with it.

In particular, you need to get two things straight:

1. *It is not about you.* Don't take it personally. The people getting upset don't hate you, or your mother, or your football team; they are just upset that things are different.
2. *You may not need them.* Figure out if you can/want/need to get them on board with what you are doing.

We had an email the other day from a cool teacher who was playing dance music in-between classes and encouraging kids to have a little dance party so that they would exercise and also enjoy the day. He received a horrible barrage of emails from fellow teachers who couldn't believe he could be so stupid and rude.

These types of blockers (or 'resistant followers', as we call them) come out of the woodwork when you make change. We call them resistant followers because we are convinced that everyone will be on board with the idea soon, they just don't know it yet!

These resistant followers come in all flavours.

There is Al Ready. He has seen it all before and tells you that your idea has already been tried years ago and found wanting. With Al, ask him what went wrong the first time around, and get his advice on how things can go differently this time.

There might be a Charity Case and her friend Mona Lisa, who can't possibly take on any more work. Beat them to their moaning and acknowledge how amazing they are for battling through all the tough times and still delivering great work. What legends.

May Belater would love to help—just after reporting is finished, or when the in-laws head home or when the weather warms up. To help with this, set artificial deadlines for the team, and celebrate loudly when you hit them.

Then there is Con Ceited, who has everything figured out and doesn't need your help. Bring him into the team, and say quietly something like, 'I am giving you a super-tough job, but I need my best person on this'.

And don't forget Chip Shoulder, who just really, really doesn't like you. No problems; let someone else be the face of the project, so Chip won't care as much.

You need to acknowledge that these people exist, and then use your best judgement as an edupreneur to determine if you are going to work to try to win them over, or simply just ignore them.

Remember—the ultimate comeback to any argument is doing what people said couldn't be done.

(Sherrel Bergmann and Judith Brough have done some awesome work in this area. For more great tips on dealing with blockers, check out their book *Lead Me, I Dare You!*)

Resilience

Coming up against blockers is tough. Your days become longer and you feel like your back is up against the wall and everyone is out to get you.

The best edupreneurs keep listening, improving and fighting their way relentlessly though challenges.

Dave had been working for six months on one idea in a school he ran, when the state director called him and told him that he couldn't go ahead with it. Rather cheekily, he gave the director two alternatives. Let him do it, or fire him. But he also said that if his idea didn't work, he would fall on his sword and take the blame in the media.

Doing this kind of stuff takes big resilience.

The trouble is, resilience is pretty poorly understood as a term. It does not mean just stubbornly pushing through challenges. The word actually comes from the Latin root word *resiliens*, which means 'to bounce back'.

Resilience is when you are massively knocked down by something, being able to get back on your feet, dust yourself off, learn from the experience and then come back to fight better the next day.

As our good friend Jeff Li, a maths teacher in Harlem, says, 'Forgive yourself every night, and recommit every morning'.

So, our edupreneurial friends, when the challenges come your way—which they will—bounce back, learn from the experience and keep trying to make change. Many others around the world will be doing the very same thing that very same day.

Run your own conference

When we get asked to speak at a school, many of the briefings are the same: 'Our team is quite tired and they need a burst of inspiration'.

We often try to talk the school into running its own conference, drawing speakers from the teachers at the school and training them up to tell their ideas in a powerful, inspiring and compelling way. It is always amazing to watch what happens when a teaching group has that moment of 'We have got this, and we are an awesome team!'

So think about doing something like this in your school.

For the next professional development day coming up, don't hire any outside experts or thought leaders. Block out the day, invite people to apply if they want to get on stage and then curate a list of around ten speakers. (Maybe sneak yourself on to the speakers list so you can get your idea out there as well.)

Get the first five to present their ideas in seven minutes, and then ask the audience to choose which session they want to dive deeper into.

Then do another round of this.

You can then use some of the tools in this book for the final session of the day to see what your staff can come up with.

(And you can spend all the money you would have spent on an 'expert' on awesome food, or donate it to a local charity!)

Scaling beyond your school

So maybe you are feeling pretty good about your idea.

You reckon that it is getting some great results for kids.

You have got past the blockers and lots of people are really happy about what you have created.

Now you want to share it with other schools in your town or city.

We see edupreneurs that we work with do this all the time and it is awesome to watch.

They start building networks on Twitter and speaking at local conferences and TeachMeets, presenting their ideas to regional leaders and politicians and making noise in the media.

They bring people along with them, mobilising champions in schools all around the place.

They separate their names from the product, choosing to scale the idea, rather than get the glory themselves. And they make an awesome difference.

Are you up for this?

If so, read on!

1. What am I passionate about?
2. We believe...
3. But right now the reality is...
4. What are the root causes?
5. Other players?
6. Focus on one root cause.
7. Ideate fifty solutions.
8. Prototype the best two.
9. Test the best.
10. Pivot or persevere.
11. Turn the idea into something real.
12. **Prove it gets results.**

Making pudding with proof in it

If you want to take your idea beyond your school, you need to have a really clear idea of the kind of impact it has.

We love, love, love collecting impact data, but always keep things really simple.

So, a couple of things to think about.

The first is the difference between outputs and outcomes.

An output is something that you do. For example, 'We conducted eight parent evenings this year', or 'Children read 18 000 pages from 'books this year'.

An outcome is what happened — the result of these actions.

In other words, an output is you teaching a lesson. The outcome is kids learning it.

If our output was that we conducted eight parent evenings this year, our outcome might be that we saw significantly increased engagement of parents for sixty-two of our children.

Or if our output was children read 18 000 pages from books this year, our outcome might be that we improved reading levels for 126 students, by three levels above the expected growth.

Uncovering a program's impact can be a really complex task, and a team of academics could spend a year in your school delving into a whole raft of metrics. Of course, you need to report on lots of areas in a school and this requirement only increases as you move into positions of greater leadership, but for a change project we suggest keeping things really simple.

So to bring your outputs and outcomes together in a simple way you could use the sentence: *[Number of kids/staff / parents and so on]* engaged with *[our output]*, which helped result in *[the outcomes for the number of kids]*.

So, for example:

> We ran eight parent evenings this year in our Proud Parents program and the parents of ninety-seven children came along to at least one meeting. *[output]*
>
> This has helped us significantly improve parent engagement for sixty-two students. *[outcomes]*
>
> This information was provided by evidence from the surveys the parents filled out during the evenings.

You need to be able to put your hand on your heart and say, when we started our numbers were like this; now, because of this project, our numbers are this. But don't take all of the credit.

You might notice in the sentences we used 'helped'. This word is an important one. Chances are, lots of things happened in the school in a year to help improve parent engagement or reading scores. Your project might have really helped, but you might ruffle a few feathers if you take all the credit. The desire to attribute the outcomes to just your outputs is a strong one, but stay humble, and acknowledge that your idea is just part of the team's efforts.

Also, while numbers are great, people remember stories. When you are messaging your impact, feel free to throw in some anecdotal evidence that shows your project is making a difference. It could be something like:

> A parent, who had never come to a parent evening, came along to our fifth meeting. She had a great time and personally thanked me at the end of the night. She is now a volunteer and cooks the BBQ for us every month!

Or

> A student who had never finished a book before fell in love with the Harry Potter series during the reading month. He read every single book in the series and raised his reading scores by ten levels this year.

The more you can reinforce your data by providing some more 'meat', the better. So talk to students. Conduct surveys. Look at their academic results. Monitor their attendance rates. Be creative in what kind of impact data you collect, but remember to keep on fattening the pig, rather than just spending all of your time weighing it.

Angels and evangelists

Evangelists get a bad rap these days—with their bleached white teeth, expensive suits, private jets and corny TV shows.

But the word 'evangelist' is actually really cool. It means 'one who brings the good news'.

The bestselling author Guy Kawasaki worked at Apple in the early days and his business card used to read 'Apple Evangelist'. His job each day was to tell people how great the Apple Macintosh was.

If you want to scale your idea beyond your school, you are going to need evangelists to help you do this. Who can you find and inspire to fall in love with your program and maybe start to roll it out in their school?

Where evangelists spread the word for you, angels are the ones who open doors for you. They are the decision-makers who hold the keys to the castle—they can pick up the phone and hook things up, or encourage other principals to take your idea on board.

Find out who you need to recruit as angels and evangelists, and do everything you can to keep them on board and excited about what you are doing.

Pitch me

Second to having a great program, your pitch is one of the most important pieces in your toolkit as a fellow changemaker. This is how you get people backing you. When we say a 'pitch', we mean a sixty-second summary of your idea that is inspiring and compelling, and excites people to get involved. When someone says, 'So tell me about this project', this is them saying, 'Pitch me your idea'.

Your pitch needs to be:

- *Complete:* Is all the important stuff is in there? As Steve Jobs said, strip away the unnecessary so the necessary can be heard.
- *Concise:* Experts often recommend the 'elevator pitch', meaning you need to be able to get all the important info across in sixty seconds. According to literary legend, Hemingway was once asked to write a story in six words that made the room cry. He succeeded with the words, 'For Sale. Baby Shoes. Never Worn'.
- *Clear:* Can you strip out any lingo, jargon or TLAs (three-letter acronyms)? They may make sense to you and some people in the room, but chances are you will lose other people.
- *Compelling:* Are people leaning in? Are they interested in your solution? Is this a big problem that they are really happy someone is solving?
- *Credible:* Are you coming across as the kind of person who can nail this? You can't always give them your CV, but credibility comes across in the way you speak, and the passion you have as you present your ideas.
- *Contextualised:* Is the problem and your solution relevant to the people you are pitching to?
- *Consistent:* Are you able to nail your pitch every time, speaking clearly about what you do?
- *Conversational:* Are you having a chat, or just throwing your ideas at people?
- *Closed:* Do you have a clear ask at the end? Is there a way that they can help? The part where you ask for something is the most important part of the pitch.

1. What am I passionate about?
2. We believe...
3. But right now the reality is...
4. What are the root causes?
5. Other players?
6. Focus on one root cause.
7. Ideate fifty solutions.
8. Prototype the best two.
9. Test the best.
10. Pivot or persevere.
11. Turn the idea into something real.
12. Prove it gets results.
13. Make it scalable and sustainable.

Getting ready for scale

If you are thinking about taking your idea to serious scale, you will need to consider a couple of things:

1. *Is your program sustainable?* If it is costing you a fortune to get results, chances are other people are not going to take the idea on. Get creative and work hard to drive the cost of your program down.
2. *Is it scalable?* You were likely a key player in making this program a success. But when we take you out of the picture, can the program still be run? When something is scalable, you can open other sites exponentially if you choose, without too much trouble.

Oh, and one more thing. Is your program ten times better than the other solutions that are out there? Because change is tough, people will often only jump to a new program or idea if it is dramatically better than others they're already trying. Is yours?

If you have all of these things sorted, awesome! You are getting ready for growth.

What kind of impact are we talking about here?

Okay.

So you have figured out that you have a cool idea and schools in your region are taking it on board.

Now you need to ask yourself a big, big question.

How far do you want to take this? Is this something that could change the lives of thousands, or even millions of children?

Remember in the Dream section, where we completed the sentence, 'We believe in a school/community/country/world where ...'?

Now we are going to give you something to think about.

Do you want to revise that statement?

At EC, our 'We believe' statement says, 'We believe in a world where every child has a great teacher, every school has a great leader, and every community has a great school'. It is a big challenge.

Paul Polak, a guy who has brought 25 million people out of poverty, says, 'If your idea won't change one million lives, don't bother taking it to scale'. That's a pretty big challenge.

If you want to think big like this, strap in and get ready for the ride of your life.

Scale ideas

As Eleanor Roosevelt said, 'Small minds discuss people. Average minds discuss events. Great minds discuss ideas'. One thing that is important to make clear is that we are not talking about scaling *you*; we are talking about scaling your idea.

Scaling does not mean you stretching yourself thin and trying to launch and lead more programs; instead, it means thinking cleverly about how the most people can benefit from your idea.

Stanford professors and authors Robert Sutton and Huggy Rao give an amazing example of this in the '100 000 Lives Campaign', led by Joe McCannon.

It was all very simple, really. They came up with a list of proven methods that reduced the number of unnecessary deaths in hospitals in the United States. If a hospital in one part of the country was excellent at reducing deaths during and after heart surgery, for example, Joe's team would figure out what they were doing right and then spread the idea nationally.

As the campaign grew, doctors were calling in to radio shows, sharing things frankly and spreading the idea that errors and risks could be reduced with a few simple changes to the way things were done.

As they scaled these ideas across the country, they started to see shifts in the number of deaths being reported by hospitals. They were living up to their bold name of '100 000 Lives.'

This is awesome stuff, and a great example of scaling an idea, rather than an individual.

In favour of taking something to scale

Imagine you discover a vaccine for the Ebola virus.

You have two choices.

Firstly, you could keep it quiet. Maybe you invite a few friends over, bring your closest family members together, swear them all to secrecy and then give them the vaccination. They are personally protected from this scary thing forever.

Or, you could share your discovery with the world.

You could let people know that you have this incredible vaccine, and get some really smart people to join your team to help figure out a way to vaccinate the whole world and wipe this horrible virus off the planet.

Which option would you take?

We know our answer.

Against taking something to scale

So, at the start of the book we said that making change in schools is simple. We stick by that, but we do want to warn you: if you want to take your idea from having an impact on hundreds of kids, to having an impact on millions of kids, it is tough work. Very tough.

If you want to take your idea to massive scale, here is what you need to prepare yourself for:

- years of work
- lots of people saying NO to you all the time
- doubters, haters and critics
- nasty things written about you in the media
- sleepless nights
- your doctor, partner and friends saying, 'You should really take a holiday'.

If you don't want this, and want to keep your vision at 'We believe in a school where . . .', that is amazing.

If you are willing to take all of this on with the hopes that you can change the game for a huge number of kids, keep reading. (Or if you are just curious, keep reading as well.)

But I am a teacher, not an entrepreneur!

Marcus Veerman was an outdoor education teacher who spent the first few years of his career taking kids outside the four walls of their classrooms and teaching them about the world in the great outdoors. He passionately believed that kids could learn so much through play and adventure.

A few years into his career, his wife secured a volunteer position to work in a school on the Thailand–Burma border. He went along, ready for an adventure and a change of scenery. While he was there, the organisation his wife was working at asked if he could build a playground for the kids.

He got to work and, two weeks later, they cut the ribbon on their first playground. He loved seeing the wonder on the children's faces. A week later, the teachers told him the children were attending more and concentrating better, and seemed happier. The teachers admitted that they were less stressed too and, as a result, had more energy to teach better. Then a local principal asked if Marcus could build another one for the school in the next village. The children and staff at that school loved their playground too.

So then Marcus put up some posters in the local cyber cafes and gathered a team of volunteers. Over the next two years, with the local education charities, they built forty playgrounds across the region, in very poor communities and sometimes even for kids in refugee camps.

Marcus and his team were operating on a lean budget and making the playgrounds from old tires, forty-gallon drums and other local materials.

The kids loved them, and so did the teachers.

But Marcus and his team got really tired. After they opened the fortieth playground he was admitted to hospital, completely exhausted and suffering from all sorts of nasty bugs. He had literally worn himself into the ground.

He had lost his mojo.

He and his wife handed the project to a local charity, bought a campervan and toured around Europe for a year, thinking about their next move. Marcus wanted to keep making playgrounds but he had to think of a smarter way to scale his idea.

They returned home to Australia inspired and energised, and got to work, creating a website where anyone from around the world could log on, start a project, raise a small amount of money, and then learn how to build an awesome playground from local materials.

It used to take Marcus and his team two full weeks of work to build a playground. Now one of his playgrounds is built somewhere in the world every day, just by someone visiting his site. In fact, as you read this, 350 000 kids will be playing on one of his playgrounds.

Amazing.

Do you think Marcus would ever have thought he could have such an impact when he built that first playground all those years ago?

(If you would like to know more about Marcus and his playgrounds, check out playgroundideas.org.)

Ways to scale

So, you're still thinking that you want to scale your idea across the world. Here are some ways that you could do it:

- *Like a hippy:* You give the idea away for free. You send free resources to people, set up a great website, speak at events. People can take the idea wherever they want to take it, and you give away control.
- *Like McDonald's:* You franchise your idea, selling your project all around the place. All the sites look pretty similar and are guided by a pretty clear rule book.
- *Like a Chinese restaurant:* Chinese (or any national cuisine, really) restaurants pop up all over the world, and while many of them look pretty similar, no central body is telling them what to do (like with McDonald's). So this is where you franchise your idea, allowing your project to start up everywhere, but not controlling it too tightly.
- *Like a Silicon Valley startup:* You raise loads of cash, build a team and go for it.
- *With someone else:* You find another group, with people who are weak where you are strong, and strong where you are weak, and you do something cool together.

Some of these ideas require you stepping out of the classroom as a teacher and growing your idea in a different way. Guidance on how to do this is something for a different book!

Changing the system

A big 'smart cut' to taking your idea to scale is to change the system. As someone who played at the system level for a while, here are Dave's tips for you to keep in mind if you decide to take this approach:

1. *Keep it simple:* If you create an idea that is incredibly complex to replicate and implement, I can assure you it will not be adopted by the system. Even if the strategy behind your idea is complex, make sure that the implementation is super simple.
2. *Show lots of wins:* The wins for everyone need to be really clear. Show how the idea might create wins for teachers, parents, politicians and the community and most importantly, you need to show big outcomes for the students. Make the case so compelling to everyone involved that it would be crazy not to roll the idea out.
3. *Make it cost effective:* You might think your idea is great and making lots of impact. But if it costs ridiculous amounts of money, time and resources to roll out, it will not be adopted by the system.
4. *Build your champions:* Your idea will only go on to see change at a system level if you have champions. These are the people of influence who become raving fans of your idea and lobby for you. They have the keys to the gates and know who you need to talk to. Find these champions and thrill them.
5. *Let it go:* One of the biggest impediments to your idea changing the system is, funnily enough, you. Sometimes we hold on too tightly to our ideas because we want to get the accolades for them. If you don't care who gets the credit for something, amazing things can be achieved.

You can't do this alone

If you want to scale way beyond your school or your state, you cannot do it alone. You need to build a team.

Every team needs visionaries (the dreamers with the big ideas), thinkers (the people who can play devil's advocate and also analyse the situation) and doers (the people who go out and get things done).

Focus your efforts on finding doers. You can be the dreamer — and there is never a shortage of devil's advocates. You can always find plenty of people who can tell you what not to do!

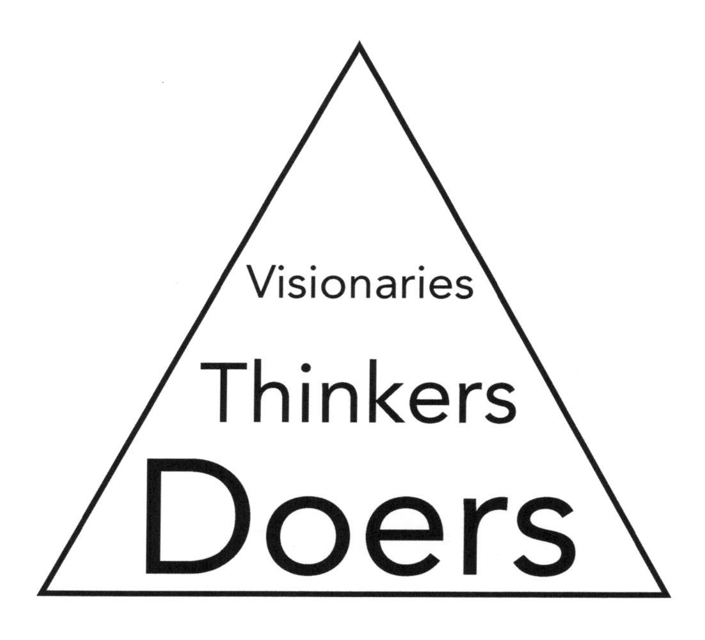

Getting the right people on the bus

So you know you need a team, but where do you start?

With the people you know—the teachers from your school, the people you engage with on Twitter and the parents who care about this idea as much as you do.

Chances are, you don't have millions of dollars to go out and hire a superstar cast of experts, so you need to start by mobilising volunteers or people who will work very cheaply for you.

At this point, get super-clear on what kind of people you need in your core team. To use a military metaphor, don't try to build an army of volunteers; instead, build a 'special forces' team—people focused and trained on specific tasks.

Also hire people for culture. If you wouldn't want to grab a drink with someone or spend your Saturday morning with them, don't bring them into your team.

Try to bring in a mix of old friends and strangers. You don't just want 'yes' people who bring you the same old ideas.

Finally, don't spend huge amounts of time giving people big long orientations and lots of training when they join. Instead, bring them into the team, see how they do and then, if they are awesome, start to give them more of your attention.

Keeping them on the bus

Building a team is often the easy part; keeping them is really tough. And not being able to pay anyone in the early days makes it even tougher!

So here are our tips for keeping your awesome team as you grow your impact:

- *Think big with your team but act small.* Have a big vision and keep telling each other that you are going to change the world. But know what you have to do today to move closer to that vision. And celebrate each incremental step along the way.
- *Don't work long; work smart.* Don't do boring meetings with minutes, secretaries and formalities. Get your team of doers together, do good work and, when you are done, take it easy and let people go home.
- *Align people with the stuff they are good at and what they care about.* If you make your introvert the MC of your next event, they will quit. Push your people, but with support.
- *Thank them.* All the time.
- *Have fun!* If working in your team is the best part of their week, people will keep coming back.
- *Remember that the only thing more powerful than ownership is authorship.* If you let your team write the plan, they will make it happen.

Leadership versus management

As an edupreneur leading this venture, sometimes you need to lead your team and sometimes you have to manage them.

Here is a pretty simple way to understand the difference between the two.

Imagine your team is stuck in the middle of the Amazon jungle. It is hot, sweaty and tough going. Your team doesn't know if you are going to make it out alive.

You're trying to slice your way through the thick jungle to get back to the ship that's going to take you home.

When you are managing, you are making sure the team's bush knives are sharp, the team is fed and that they keep going through the jungle.

When you lead, you climb a tree, figure out which direction the ocean is and then come down and inspire and inform the team about where they need to head. It is your job to figure out how much of your time you spend up the tree and how much you spend down in the jungle with your team.

Remember—you can learn to become a better leader. Many people thought that a young Mark Zuckerberg was not going to be able to lead a growing Facebook. He turned down a $1 billion buyout from Yahoo and many people thought he was crazy. But that young CEO has turned into one of the best in Silicon Valley, at the helm of a company worth tens of billions of dollars.

Ssshh! Listen

As you take all this to scale, make sure your head doesn't get too big and that you keep listening to the people you are providing solutions for.

Keep taking time out to sit down with them.

Be like CEO of Air New Zealand, Christopher Luxon, who spends one day every month serving as a flight attendant so he can stay in touch with what is happening on his planes.

Keep asking students, teachers and parents what they like about your program.

How do they wish it were better?

Step through their user experience as they engage with your program. How could you reduce the pain points and increase the pleasure points?

Have you ever walked into an Apple or Nespresso store? You feel pretty great, don't you? They have figured out every little detail to make sure they are getting the result they want (for you to buy stuff you don't need, in this case!).

How can you continue to thrill your users like these big companies do?

1. What am I passionate about?
2. We believe...
3. But right now the reality is...
4. What are the root causes?
5. Other players?
6. Focus on one root cause.
7. Ideate fifty solutions.
8. Prototype the best two.
9. Test the best.
10. Pivot or persevere.
11. Turn the idea into something real.
12. Prove it gets results.
13. Make it scalable and sustainable.
14. Take it to scale and change many lives.

Making a magnificent noise

If you are trying to scale this program, you need to start thinking about how you want to get your idea out to the world. More specifically, though, you need to figure out who needs to hear about it.

Imagine you walk into a huge cocktail party with a thousand guests. Somewhere in that room are people who really need your program. But they are hidden among all of the people who don't care about your program because it doesn't solve any of their problems.

If you just walked into the room and talked loudly and aimlessly about what you are doing as you walked around, you probably wouldn't find the people you are looking for.

Perhaps you could find a well-connected person who could tell you where the important people are for you. Or you could wear a t-shirt that says, 'Hey, do you have this problem? I can help!' Or you could try to get on stage during the speeches and chat about what you are doing for a minute.

It is the same in the real world, outside of the cocktail party.

The media can be an awesome friend for you as you grow your program. Give them good stories and help them write positive things about what is happening in the community.

On social media, reach out to the key connectors who can make noise for you.

Get on stage at the conferences where lots of people are facing the problem that you have solved.

Find the people at the party who want to talk to you, and say hi.

OUR REALLY GREAT IDEA

Media

Blogs

Twitter

Fans

Conferences

Building a movement

Your idea needs to go way beyond just you.

If you want to move this beyond your school, you need to build a movement.

You need to create something so great that, if you decided to quit, a line of people would be ready to take it way further than you ever could.

Have you seen Derek Siver's video of the shirtless dancing guy? In the video, Derek discusses how movements aren't really started by leaders — they are actually started when a 'lone nut' finds their first followers.

Let's say, heaven forbid, that you get hit by a bus tomorrow. Actually, that is too scary. Let's go with something less likely. Imagine you get mauled by a hippopotamus tomorrow (they are the most dangerous mammals in Africa, by the way). What would happen? Would someone else pick up the mantle and run with it — and maybe even do a better job than you?

Do you have your first follower yet?

The most important person in all this

Yes, you are passionate about your work.

Yes, getting your program out there is important.

But you should keep one thing right at the front of your thinking.

Your idea is never more important than your life, and your loved ones.

Your health and wellbeing, and your relationships with those closest to you, are the ultimate trump card. If you lose their support or lose your health, all of your grand ideas come crashing down. It's hard to lead others when you can't lead yourself.

Look after yourselves, friends!

Sleep. Eat well. Meditate. Stay fit. Unplug. Slow down. Get re-inspired.

Smile.

Have fun.

Final bits

1. What am I passionate about?

2. We believe...

3. But right now the reality is...

4. What are the root causes?

5. Other players?

6. Focus on one root cause.

7. Ideate fifty solutions.

8. Prototype the best two.

9. Test the best.

10. Pivot or persevere.

11. Turn the idea into something real.

12. Prove it gets results.

13. Make it scalable and sustainable.

14. Take it to scale and change many lives.

15. Return to step 1 or retire.

Retire, or return to step 1

So when does your career as an edupreneur stop (or start)? That's totally up to you.

Remember the Greensboro Four guys and how they all went back to drink a coffee in the same cafeteria when they were old men? We say, if you reach a moment like that you have two options.

Option 1 is where you call it a day, and move to a house by the beach or in the mountains, and live in peace.

Option 2 is where you return to step 1 on the journey and determine what it is that you are most passionate about now. Oh, and by the way, your age shouldn't heavily feature in your decision-making; just check out these cats:

- At twenty-two, Thomas Edison created his first invention — an electric vote recorder.
- At thirty-eight, Neil Armstrong set foot on the moon.
- At thirty-six, Marie Curie shared the Nobel Prize in Physics (and at forty-four won the Nobel Prize in Chemistry).
- At fifty, Charles Darwin wrote *Origin of the Species.*
- At sixty-two, JRR Tolkien published the first volume of his fantasy series The Lord of the Rings.
- At seventy-two, Margaret Ringenberg completed the around-the-world air race.
- At ninety-five, Nola Ochs graduated from college with a Bachelor of Arts.

Remember — today is the oldest you have ever been and the youngest you'll ever be again.

Smell the roses

As an edupreneur taking an idea to scale, you will work harder than most.

You will get told no, all the time.

You will fail.

You will be criticised.

But the negatives will all be worth it because you are changing lives.

You are helping kids grab a hold of their futures and head in a direction that they want to go in.

Every now and then, take a few minutes out to imagine your kids twenty years from now. Imagine them healthy, and as great mothers and fathers. In jobs they love. Giving back to their communities.

This is the ultimate reward for all of us in the work we do.

Remember—the word 'education' comes from Latin *educatio*, which means a bringing up, or a rearing—to lead out.

So each day we come to work, let's keep that meaning at the forefront. Are we leading our kids out of childhood and into magnificent futures as best we can? If the answer is yes, then it was most certainly another day worth living.

Never forget the one in the many

After a year at the school they had been running in East Africa, Aaron and Kaitlin were set to return to Kenya to help grow the capacity of an orphanage and education project. As they packed their bags on their final night, they had a lot to celebrate.

The school looked fantastic, and had been fixed up, landscaped and painted by the kids. A global bank had come on as a donor and the library and science lab were filled with great books and equipment. Attendance had lifted to 90 per cent and their staff had grown from the school's lowest point of only three teachers to eight brilliant educators who came to work every day passionate about helping the kids. The farms were growing crops that the kids were eating daily and the students were running a wide range of businesses to contribute to the running of the school and also help them save for studies after high school. Aaron and Kaitlin's goal on their first night had been to get ten kids through the national exams; fourteen had succeeded that year, with some students successfully enrolled in architecture and law at a local university.

Aaron and Kaitlin wanted to travel light back to Kenya and so had been giving much of what they owned away to students and community members. For some reason, their old t-shirts had been the most popular items.

Kaitlin had invited a student called Thea over for a cup of tea. The two of them had been very close that year and Kaitlin wanted to give Thea a small gift. As Thea sat on the outside porch with Kaitlin, she peered into their house, looking for the t-shirt that she was expecting Kaitlin to give to her. After a few minutes of small talk, Kaitlin held out a necklace to Thea, with the word 'rafiki' (Swahili for friend) inscribed on it. Thea took a look at the necklace, and then looked up at Kaitlin and said, 'Sister Kait, the necklace is nice, but do you have any t-shirts left over?' Kaitlin had no more t-shirts, but they kept chatting, sharing tea and then Thea headed back to her dormitory to sleep.

A few minutes after she had gone, Kaitlin asked Aaron a simple question.

'Are we nothing more than a t-shirt to these kids? After everything we have done, including almost dying here a few times, have we made a difference here this year?'

Aaron didn't have an answer for Kaitlin, but was saved by another knock at the door.

It was Frank.

He was an amazing kid, from a very poor family. He had worked hard all year and had passed his exams. But Aaron was tired, and the question from Kaitlin had thrown him. On answering the door, he shook his head and said, 'Sorry, Frank. No more t-shirts, my friend.'

Frank held up his hand to interrupt Aaron.

'I didn't come for a t-shirt, Mr Aaron,' he said, tears in his eyes. 'I came to say thank you to you and Sister Kait for changing my life.'

And then he walked away into the darkness.

Aaron closed the door quietly, tears in his eas well. He turned around to look at Kaitlin. 'It was worth it,' she said.

So, our edupreneurial friends: what you do is worth it. And even though we have spent the last section of this book talking about taking ideas to scale and impacting millions of lives, know that there are many Franks out there who you have affected in incredibly powerful ways. And even if there is only one, it is all worth it.